DRAGONS vs. EAGLES

Wales vs. America
in the Boxing Ring

D1477164

GARETH JONES

ST DAVID'S PRESS

Cardiff

Published in Wales by St. David's Press, an imprint of
Ashley Drake Publishing Ltd
PO Box 733
Cardiff
CF14 7ZY
www.st-davids-press.com

First Impression – 2014

ISBN 978-1-902719-38-2

British Library Cataloguing-in-Publication Data.
A CIP catalogue for this book is available from the British Library.

CONTENTS

CONTENTS

ACKNOWLEDGEMENTS

I must express my gratitude to those living boxers who helped with the writing of this book. I also owe much to those long-gone reporters whose eye-witness accounts have allowed me to flesh out the stories of fights from distant eras.

Many of the photographs included have been shared by the boxers involved and their families, but I must also acknowledge the generosity of *Boxing News*, Matchroom Boxing, the Huw Evans Picture Agency (www. huwevansimages.com), Jane Warburton (www.saddoboxing.com), Robert Haines (www.roberthaines.com), Philip Sharkey, Howard Evans, Wynford Jones and Dave Furnish.

INTRODUCTION

As a small country, Wales has always punched above its weight in the ring. And while the United States, with 100 times the population, are the giants of world boxing, St David has done surprisingly well against Goliath over the years.

There was the dazzling skill of Jim Driscoll, the man from Cardiff's docklands, whose ability so entranced American observers that the gunfighter-turned-journalist, Bat Masterson, dubbed him 'Peerless'. The lesson he handed out to world featherweight king Abe Attell has passed into legend, along with his rejection of a rematch with the title at stake, because he had given his word that he would appear at a charity event in his home city.

Equally popular with his native people was Tommy Farr, the charismatic heavyweight from the Rhondda, where nobody slept on the August night when he challenged the one-and-only Joe Louis for the greatest prize in sport. Crowded around crackling wireless sets, they were transfixed by the commentary from New York's Yankee Stadium and, if the result was not what they hoped for, the local hero's performance against the 'Brown Bomber' made a valley proud.

More recently, Joe Calzaghe finally convinced the transatlantic doubters by outclassing their new wonder boy, Jeff Lacy, before ending his stellar career by invading America and seeing off hall-of-famers Bernard Hopkins and Roy Jones, Jr.

As well as the big title showdowns, Wales and the US have come face to face in numerous other memorable clashes, many of which are chronicled here. Drawn from more than a century of ring history, they tell of victories and defeats and, on occasion, tragedy.

Such was the case when the 'Merthyr Matchstick', Johnny Owen, fell into a coma in his challenge to world champion Lupe Pintor, never regaining consciousness. Yet even this episode had a heartwarming sequel, when Pintor flew to Wales to unveil a statue in commemoration of his unfortunate rival.

Pintor, of course, was Mexican, but the bout took place in Los Angeles and must have its place in any chronicle of this kind. Similarly, the parameters of eligibility have been elastic enough to include a few more "outsiders" who plied their trade in the US.

I hope these recollections of time past – whether familiar or fresh to the reader's eye – will be of interest and underline how often one tiny nation has held its own against the big boys.

GARETH JONES

July 2014

1

★★★

JOHN **O'BRIEN**	vs.	FRANK **CRAIG**

OCTOBER 8, 1894	**National Sporting Club, London**

★★★

The National Sporting Club were the undisputed masters of boxing in the years which saw it emerge from the shadows and become a legal and regulated activity. Its members and guests were drawn from an elite whose right to run everything from the affairs of state to the throwing of punches was unquestioned in those days of Empire.

Those who provided their entertainment were from the other end of society's ladder.

Frank Craig had arrived in this world on April Fools' Day about a quarter of a century earlier, although the whereabouts are uncertain. It may have been Columbus, Georgia, or the Ohio city of the same name. Then again some say he was born in New York. He definitely grew up there, earning the ring name 'The Harlem Coffee Cooler'.

American society was just as stratified as that in Victorian Britain and Craig, son of a black Cuban father and a Native American mother, found himself disputing the "coloured middleweight championship" against a Philadelphian, Joe Butler, losing inside two rounds. When they met again a year later, Frank outpointed his rival and claimed the crown – even though the contest was only a four-rounder. He never defended, heading across the Atlantic, where prospects for a black fighter were less restricted.

His reputation was such that he was invited to make his British bow before the club's aristocratic patrons at their Covent Garden headquarters. In the opposite corner was someone who had already established himself as a favourite there.

John O'Brien was born to Irish parents in the Cardiff docklands district of Newtown, known as 'Little Emerald Isle',

John O'Brien

Frank Craig, who loved apple dumplings

but grew up in the Roath area, where his street-fighting skills had led him to more formal encounters in the booths that travelled the country's fairgrounds.

Competing at a time when boxing in "the old style" – that is, with bare fists – was still in vogue, John knocked out a Rhondda pugilist, Jack Jones, known as 'Shoni Engineer', to claim the Welsh middleweight title. Both men were arrested afterwards and bound over to keep the peace.

Not that O'Brien was bothered. He graduated to the gloved version and was soon patrolling the London rings and establishing himself as the best in England, too. He even signed a contract to travel to New Orleans and challenge world champion Bob Fitzimmons, only for a bout of sciatica to sideline him for two years, wrecking his dream.

The disappointment, coupled with his recurring illness, brought a casual attitude to training and when he was matched with the visiting American, John had to shed three stone (42lb) in 18 days. It left him in no state to handle the fit and fast Craig over a scheduled 20 rounds.

Frank soon realised that he had little to beat. He floored the Welshman at the end of the first and his thoughts turned to his stomach. The landlady at his lodgings had promised him apple dumplings for supper; in the corner, he asked that she be sent a telegram. "Start baking," it said. "I will not be long delayed." He finished off poor John in the next session.

The pair were to meet again six months later, also at the NSC, though it had not been planned. Craig was matched with another Welshman, Ted Pritchard, but the Merthyr-born Londoner was taken ill on the night and O'Brien was dragged from a nearby pub to replace him. So drunk he could barely stand, John somehow made it through the first round and promptly retired.

The fiasco ruined him as an attraction and he went home to Cardiff, working on the docks until rheumatism and alcohol combined to kill him at the age of 43.

Craig headed back to the US in 1899, losing a world title showdown to Johnny Ryan in New York, before returning to settle in London. He toured the country – including fights in Newport and Neath – and regularly featured in the music halls with a tap-dancing routine in which he accompanied himself on the mouth-organ.

He put his earnings into several pubs – not in the same way as John O'Brien – and loved to flaunt his wealth, parading with his white wife in an open carriage, his expensive suits adorned with a diamond "as big as a locomotive headlight". Unlike Jack Johnson back in his homeland, the Brits loved him for it. He died in his seventies in his adopted city.

 **2**

FREDDIE **WELSH**	vs.	PACKEY **McFARLAND**

FEBRUARY 21, 1908	**Hippodrome, Milwaukee**

The man who bore his nationality as his ring name was building quite a reputation in the country where he planned to make his fortune. But even as he became popular with American fight fans, he was still a visitor from foreign parts - and sometimes that was made pretty obvious.

Frederick Hall Thomas was unusual in many ways. Unlike most of his countrymen, he did not come up from the pit to seek a career in the ring; the son of a Pontypridd auctioneer, he came from a family affluent enough to send him to fee-paying schools.

He was also an avid reader, who was to cultivate the acquaintance of authors - he was said to have been the inspiration for Scott Fitzgerald's antihero, Jay Gatsby - while he anticipated modern sportsmen in paying close attention to his diet.

But his middle-class background and tendencies were not obvious when he learned to scrap on the campsites he shared with other itinerant workers after first crossing the Atlantic as a 16-year-old. When he graduated to the more organised fight game, Freddie demonstrated an outstanding talent and when he returned home in 1907 his fellow-countrymen had their chance to see what the fuss was all about.

His acquired accent and a perceived arrogance was less well received, however, and Welsh headed back to the US, determined to reach the top on his own terms. But he was always to be an outsider – and that

Freddie Welsh

Packey McFarland

could mean more than just his rivals to deal with.

Patrick McFarland, universally known as 'Packey', was a tough so-and-so. He needed to be to survive in the Chicago stockyards and, when he took his fists into the ring, there were few who could live with him. He was still unbeaten when he was matched with Welsh in Milwaukee, America's brewing capital, a city he knew well.

It was not simply the surroundings that were familiar to Packey. He insisted on choosing his own referee and brought one Malachy Hogan the 80-odd miles up the Lake Michigan shoreline from Chicago. Originally from Tipperary, Hogan was regarded as an honest and diligent official - apart from those occasions when one of his fellow citizens was in the ring.

Welsh might have known what to expect. Only three weeks earlier, he had beaten up a certain Charlie Neary, only for the third man to rule it a draw.

When it came to the 10-rounder with McFarland, Freddie's superior boxing was evident from the start, but in the fourth he shipped a punch below the Plimsoll Line and subsided to the floor in pain. Mr Hogan saw nothing wrong. Nor did he when the scenario was replayed in the next session.

By the eighth, however, the Welshman was in total command, opening a gash near Packey's left eye. At the final bell, the Chicago fighter was a bloody mess. Nevertheless, it was his hand raised by the seemingly shameless Hogan. Those present were in no doubt what they had witnessed. "You'll never referee another fight here while I'm mayor of Milwaukee," stormed local dignitary Sherburn Beeker.

You couldn't believe what you read in the papers, either. McFarland's manager was an experienced press agent and made sure that the reports wired to offices across the country were full of praise for his man's brilliant and, of course, deserved victory. Milwaukee's sports writers, by contrast, were unanimous: Welsh had been robbed.

In those days, of course, there was a lot of pressure on officials. Gamblers and gangsters had an unsavoury influence, while Hogan, as a businessman in the Windy City, will have been well aware of the possible consequences of what important people might consider a "wrong" decision.

Shortly after his experience in Milwaukee, the referee's health gave way. Three years later, he was dead.

3

★★

JIM		MATTY
DRISCOLL	vs.	**BALDWIN**

NOVEMBER 14, 1908	Fairmont Athletic Club, New York

★★

It was an American who gave the man from Cardiff the tag that would go down in history. But sports writer Bat Masterson, once the sheriff of Ford County, Kansas, was not always so impressed by the skills of the visitor from Wales.

British and Empire featherweight champion he may have been, but Jim Driscoll cut an unprepossessing figure in the gym. When Masterson first watched him on his arrival in the United States, he dismissed him as "the worst sample of a fighter that had ever come from England". Then he saw him in action and his views were transformed. The no-hoper became 'Peerless Jim'.

The son of Irish immigrants, Driscoll learned to box among colleagues in the composing room of a local evening paper, wrapping newsprint around his fists for impromptu sparring sessions. He progressed via the touring booths, where showman Jack Scarrott would pay him a bonus to stand on a handkerchief, hands behind his back, and defy anyone to land a punch on him.

Professional opponents found things no easier and once Jim had established his dominance at home, his eyes turned to the bounty available across the Atlantic. This was the age of the 'No Decision' bout, but the lack of an official outcome did not diminish the participants' desire and determination.

Driscoll's first public appearance came before the sportsmen of the Bronx, against a man they called 'The Bunker Hill Bearcat'. Matty Baldwin was the oldest of

'Peerless' Jim Driscoll

Matty Baldwin

14 children and left school at 15 to work as an elevator operator. It was not long before the teenage Bostonian was taking his lift to the top floor, where he would test his fighting skills against his contemporaries, while would-be customers on other levels pressed their buttons in vain. His success in those impromptu battles soon led to swapping punches for money.

And he was good. Massachusetts was one of the states where verdicts were still permitted, and they usually went his way. One victory – this time on the say-so of the press – came over a young Freddie Welsh.

He was also an inch taller and a good five pounds heavier than Driscoll. Not that Jim was ever worried by such niceties. He had dealt with many a burly brawler in the booths and, while it would have been rash to consider one of the world's top lightweights in the same category as the unfit, unskilled characters who made drink-inspired challenges on the local fairground, Baldwin's physical advantages were not a problem.

As it transpired, neither was anything else the opera-loving New Englander brought to the ring. Each blow he threw found either the smoke-filled air or the cushion of Driscoll's gloves. Among the amazed onlookers the talk was of Young Griffo, the legendary Australian still regarded by many as the greatest defensive boxer of all time.

Jim, by contrast, landed almost every time he wanted to, using the sixth and final round to demonstrate his full repertoire, with poor Matty taking one of the worst hidings of his career.

Former gunslinger Masterson was not the only reporter enchanted by the Cardiffian. "Driscoll bewildered Baldwin with his clever feinting," wrote one, "shooting in left and right with the speed of a rattlesnake's strike." Another dubbed him "one of the cleverest little fellows Johnny Bull has ever sent over", while a third summed it all up: "Matty spent six rounds shadow-boxing. Unfortunately, the shadow hit back."

When the pair met again six weeks later on the American's home ground in Boston, it was much the same. Baldwin changed tactics, boring inside and relying on hooks rather than straight punches, and it worked for the first three sessions, bringing blood from Jim's nose. But for the rest of the 12-rounder the traffic was all the other way and when referee Jack Sheehan raised the visitor's arm there was no dissent.

Matty boxed until 1916, without ever being given a title shot. Two years later, at the age of 33, he was gone, a victim of the Spanish flu epidemic that swept across North America at the end of the First World War.

4

★★★

JIM	vs.	LEACH
DRISCOLL		**CROSS**

FEBRUARY 10, 1909	**Fairmont Athletic Club, New York**

★★★

As a dentist, Leach Cross might have been expected to feel protective towards other people's teeth. Instead he moonlighted in a job which involved trying to knock them out. Perhaps he felt one method of extraction was as good as another.

With world champion Abe Attell hesitating over a date to face Driscoll, the Welshman agreed to fill time by taking on Cross in a 10-rounder at Billy Gibbon's atmospheric old venue.

Cross – real name Louis Charles Wallach, the son of Viennese Jews – was one of no fewer than eight boxing brothers raised on New York's Lower East Side, where learning to fight was a necessity for survival. But Papa Wallach was a successful businessman and young Louis was sent to university, where he qualified for his daytime profession.

He began boxing to earn a few extra bucks, changing his name to hide the activity from his parents. When an acquaintance congratulated the old man on his son's latest victory, the cat was out of the bag, but paternal wrath was calmed when he realised the size of the purse involved.

Cross became known as one of the hardest-hitting lightweights of his era. His punch had stopped the famously durable Battling Harvey inside a round, while many lesser lights had been extinguished in similarly quick time.

Leach Cross, the fighting dentist

Jim Driscoll in his prime

Leach had witnessed Driscoll's display against Matty Baldwin, but did not join in the general acclaim. He preferred to focus on Jim's lean and fragile-looking torso and imagine how much he would relish belabouring it with his dynamite-loaded fists.

Things turned out rather differently. One observer described the contest as "a combination of masterpiece and comedy", with Driscoll providing the mastery, while Cross was the unwitting comic.

There were several hitches before the first bell rang. After Cross had struggled to make 9st 9lb, Jim weighed in fully dressed – it was estimated that the American had at least a 10lb advantage. When the pair reached the ring, the home fighter protested for a good 10 minutes about the Welshman's bandages, until his own were shown to be the harder.

Once the action was under way, Leach was more subdued. The only punch he landed in the opener came after the call of 'break', while Driscoll peppered his man's nose with a succession of lefts.

Cross was rocked late in the third and his left eye began to close in the fourth, shutting completely by the seventh. When Driscoll slipped on some water in the eighth, the New Yorker took the opportunity to land a shot to the kidneys before he could rise, an act which angered the crowd until Jim signalled that he was unhurt.

The frustrated local began to insult the Welshman verbally, but was answered with a couple of blows on his open mouth, prompting laughter from ringside. Driscoll's dominance of the closing sessions was complete and the attendant journalists had a simple task in declaring him the winner.

Even Leach realised he had been in with an exceptional talent. A few days later, he came across Jim taking a nap in the gym. Cross walked over and woke him with a slap on the back, turning to his friends and grinning. "There," he said. "Now they can't say I never managed to hit Jim Driscoll."

The American boxed on until 1921, with one contest providing a delightful footnote. After Leach's fists removed several teeth from the mouth of one Knockout Brown, he put on his white coat the following day to repair the damage.

In addition to his dental practice, Cross – he legally adopted the name a year after retiring – ran a series of successful businesses, dying in 1957 at the age of 71.

5

★★★

JIM **DRISCOLL**	vs.	ABE **ATTELL**

FEBRUARY 19, 1909	National Athletic Club, New York

★★★

Fights didn't take long to arrange when boxers were ready to go to war several times a month. So it transpired that, just nine days after his masterclass against Leach Cross, Driscoll found the world featherweight champion was suddenly ready to face him.

Abe Attell had worn the crown for more than five years. 'The Little Hebrew', originally from San Francisco, had settled in New York by the time the pair came together at a packed venue on Manhattan's East 24th Street, three days before the champion turned 26. Driscoll was three years older.

Senators, supreme court judges and "it would seem, every man of prominence in New York" were among the record 4,000 in attendance. Both men scaled 8st 12½ 1b (120½ 1b) – over the feather limit, according to American rules – and the Welshman was 10 to 8 on at the start.

Abe chewed gum nonchalantly as he waited for Driscoll to join him, oozing a confidence somewhat surprising bearing in mind that he had been outpointed three months earlier by Jim's countryman, Freddie Welsh. He soon realised what he was up against.

Driscoll's elegant left hand began to beat a

Abe Attell

tattoo on Attell's features, the Californian "receiving four whacks for every one he dealt". Before the opening session had ended, Abe had touched the deck, stumbling over after his own punch had missed by feet.

This inability to land confounded Abe. "Just as he was ready to plant something upon the person of Driscoll," observed one scribe, "another left bumped his nose." The constant punishment was having its effect, with Attell's seconds having to produce a penknife to lance a swelling beneath his right eye and enable their charge to finish the 10 rounds.

The American was generally on the front foot, but that suited Jim, moving in and out and landing sharp blows as his adversary came forward. In addition, Driscoll's ability to slip punches with the slightest movement of his head frustrated Abe and had ringsiders gasping in amazement.

The Californian had his moments in the middle rounds, but Driscoll finished strongly and there was little dissent among the journalistic judges. Only one voted for Attell: ironically, it was the nickname-coining Bat Masterson. For the rest, Jim was "incomparably the better man".

The better man after the fight, as well. Despite big-bucks offers of a rematch in a jurisdiction where the title would be at stake, Jim, already booked to sail home the following day, could not be persuaded to stay around. He had promised the nuns of Nazareth House, a Catholic orphanage in Cardiff, that he would be back in time to box his customary exhibition at their annual fund-raiser.

Even though his plans had been known prior to the contest, that did not prevent the Attell camp venting their scorn. Manager Al Lippe, in particular, did not spare the vitriol, claiming Driscoll was "as yellow as a shipload of lemons" and "worried almost to death", insisting that his prior engagement was "a cheap subterfuge to escape a good lacing".

Lippe, seemingly in denial as to who had received "a good lacing" the previous evening, found little support from his fellow Americans, while, back home, Jim's townsfolk saluted him at a special dinner, presenting an illuminated address which lauded the fact that "in the midst of your triumphs in the United States you returned home to assist the cause of charity".

Driscoll went on to become the first featherweight to acquire the newly introduced Lonsdale Belt – lightweight Freddie Welsh and middle Tom Thomas had won the first two awarded, so Jim completed an incredible hat-trick for Wales – and later added the European title, but never returned to the States and that rematch with Attell.

Abe extended his reign for another three years before losing to Johnny Kilbane, boxing on until 1917. Two years later his reputation was tarnished when he was said to be the bagman for gangster Arnold Rothstein, paying Chicago White Sox baseball players to throw their World Series final with

The orphans of Nazareth House follow Driscoll's coffin through Cardiff's silent streets

Cincinnati. A compulsive gambler, the debt-laden Attell may have had little choice in the matter.

The same year saw Driscoll, already a sick man, lose his last contest to Frenchman Charles Ledoux. In January 1925 pneumonia took the 'Peerless One' at just 44. An estimated 100,000 people lined the streets of Cardiff as his funeral procession passed by; among those marching were the children of Nazareth House, honouring the man who turned his back on a world title to ensure they had a home.

6

★★

FREDDIE **WELSH**	VS.	PACKEY **McFARLAND**
MAY 30, 1910		National Sporting Club, London

★★

As Freddie, the first man to win one of the newly introduced Lonsdale Belts, was strolling down the Strand, many passers-by called out their congratulations. But it was an American voice which caught his attention.

And Packey McFarland had a proposition. Having just learned that Ad Wolgast had dethroned world lightweight champion Battling Nelson – and aware that, like his predecessor, Wolgast would be unlikely to risk his new status until he had milked its financial advantages – the Chicago man told Welsh that their best chance of making a bob or a buck was by fighting each other.

It would be their third meeting. After the sour taste left by Malachy Hogan's refereeing in Milwaukee, the pair had touched gloves five months later in a rematch at a special arena built by former heavyweight king James J. Jeffries at Vernon, just outside the Los Angeles city limits and therefore beyond the reach of the 'No Decision' rule.

The contest took place on Independence Day, while then world ruler Joe Gans was

How the trade press viewed the big fight

Welsh (right) draws McFarland on to an uppercut

defending against Nelson up the coast at San Francisco. Few expected the 'Durable Dane' to win and there were plans to name the McFarland-Welsh victor as the "white champion".

Freddie dominated the first half of the 25-round tussle and by the 15th session, the talk was that Packey needed a knockout. Then came the news that Nelson had upset the odds and Welsh seemed to lose his focus as he realised his longed-for title shot was moving further away.

McFarland took control and the last couple of sessions saw the Pontypridd man ship heavy punishment. At the end, Jeffries – if it's your own arena, you get to be referee – called it a draw. This time it was Packey who let his disappointment be known.

With Nelson, as feared, enjoying a round of theatre appearances and only occasionally venturing through the ropes, Freddie decided to head back to Britain, where he acquired both British and European titles – with the former came the first of Lord Lonsdale's ornate prizes – but the news of Wolgast's accession to the throne news put a dampener on things. McFarland was right; they needed each other.

That had been the case for a while, really, with neither getting a sniff of the championship, but a dispute over the weigh-in time – the naturally bigger Packey wanted it early to allow him to regain a few pounds – had proved insoluble. But for a showdown in Britain, where the lightweight limit was 9st 9lb (135lb), two pounds heavier than in the US, it was no longer an issue.

And the American was somewhat surprised to find that, as far as the members of the National Sporting Club were concerned, he was welcomed with more than their customary courtesy. The truculent Welsh showed insufficient deference to the club and its traditions and the game's establishment had been hoping to find someone who would shut him up.

That attitude was also reflected in the public prints, where the British writers backed McFarland while the Yanks, who regarded him as one of their own, favoured Freddie. It was a strange polarisation of views.

But whatever their opinions, those present witnessed what the new weekly *Boxing* described as "one of the most magnificent exhibitions of pure boxing ever seen". Packey, who had been expected to go for a knockout, instead displayed exceptional movement, allied to a consistent aggression which kept Welsh on the back foot. Freddie's superb defence, however, cancelled out much of McFarland's work, and he was virtually unmarked at the end of the 25 rounds, whereas the visitor's nose bled for most of the later sessions and the signs of battle were also visible around his eyes and mouth. At the end, referee Tom Scott could not separate them.

Welsh considered himself lucky. "I never fought a rottener fight in all my life," he insisted, admitting that McFarland was strong and "the finest fighter in the world".

Packey avoided comment on the verdict, preferring to praise the atmosphere. "To the end of my days I shall never forget the dandy way that crowd treated me tonight," he said. When it was suggested that the pair might clash again in America, he was righteously put out. "Why in America?" he asked. "I never wish any circumstances better than these to fight amongst."

But, with the NSC closing for its summer break, a prompt rematch was impossible. And it was never to happen, either side of the Atlantic.

Nor was McFarland ever to get his shot at the world crown, though that did not prevent him being inducted into the International Hall of Fame, five years before Welsh. He made some money, too, becoming a director of two banks before his death in 1936.

★★★

FREDDIE		WILLIE
WELSH	**VS.**	**RITCHIE**

JULY 7, 1914	**Olympia, London**

★★★

The chase was finally over. At last the Pontypridd fighter was to challenge for the world crown – and before a British crowd, at that. He had been within a whisker before: Joe Gans was going to defend against him, but was surprisingly dethroned by Battling Nelson and, while the Dane never seemed interested, his successor, Ad Wolgast, had gone so far as to agree a time and place.

That meeting was booked for November 1911 in Los Angeles, but the champion went down with appendicitis on the eve of the show. A desperate

Welsh (left) and Ritchie sign, supervised by promoter C.B. Cochran

Freddie covers up as the champion moves in

search for a stand-in came up with San Franciscan Willie Ritchie, who put up a decent show on short notice but was clearly outpointed over 20 rounds.

But now the Californian was the man with the belt. While Welsh was busy back home, adding the Empire title to his collection – he had lost and regained the British and European honours in a couple of memorable clashes with Matt Wells – Ritchie managed to obtain a shot at Wolgast, flooring the 'Michigan Wildcat' twice before winning on disqualification when Ad let slip a couple of low blows.

Freddie sailed to the US in 1913 to seek an audience with the new ruler. But Willie, like those before him, preferred a series of exhibitions and stage appearances to boost his bank account rather than risking the loss of his main selling point. When he did enter the ring it was for 'No Decision' bouts, in which his title would only be forfeit if he was knocked out. That was just as well, with one newspaper verdict going to Chicago's Charley White, who cut and battered Ritchie in the last bout before he faced Welsh.

The "Englishman", as the American press tended to refer to him, ignoring the substantial hint in his surname, had filled in time by touring Canada and parading his wares against no-hopers across the US – he boxed six times in January 1914 alone – before a deal was finally done with the champion.

C.B. Cochran, a London theatrical impresario, eventually managed to obtain the pair's signatures at a ceremony in New York, before they travelled separately to Britain, Ritchie, ironically, landing in West Wales, while Welsh disembarked at Southampton. Freddie had recently confessed that he and his "cook", Fanny, had been married for eight years; it was a necessary admission, as she was about to give birth to his daughter, Elizabeth.

Mother and child set sail as soon as they could, but by the time they reached London the baby's father was already heading for Olympia, although the crowds were so dense that he was still outside at the time the bout should have started. He had already changed, but had to rush straight from his car to the ring, with no opportunity to warm up.

Freddie began strongly, however, and wore a broad grin as he returned to the corner after the first session. As his supremacy was underlined, the odds shortened to reflect the money piling on the Welshman. Ritchie was relying heavily on his power, but his favoured uppercut was avoided so easily that one writer compared the elusive challenger to the Scarlet Pimpernel.

Willie's lips and right cheek were seeping blood from early on, but he was renowned as a slow starter and more cautious observers were careful not to celebrate too soon. In the 13th, Ritchie did indeed manage to land three successive right hooks, although Welsh was moving away, robbing them of much of their venom.

In the corner at the end of the 16th, manager Emile Thiery could be heard telling Willie that only a knockout would save the title. In his desperation, the American hurled one right hook so wild that it struck referee Eugene Corri.

Nevertheless, his efforts may well have won him the closing stages as Welsh, sure that he had done enough, focussed on defence.

Fanny and her sister, who had arrived at the hall during the fifth round, but stayed out of sight at the back, felt confident enough to slip into the ringside seats left for them. They watched some toe-to-toe exchanges in a thrilling last session before Mr Corri announced his verdict and Fanny was helped through the ropes to congratulate her husband, while the deposed Ritchie broke down and wept.

As Freddie rushed to the Waldorf to meet his little girl for the first time, the distraught American headed back to his own hotel before giving an interview to the *New York Times*. Although he complained that the arc light above the ring had dazzled him, he admitted, "Welsh earned the decision."

He could console himself with his $25,000 purse. In order to persuade the champion to travel to Britain, Freddie had agreed to take 50 per cent of the cash left over when Ritchie was paid. That proved, despite the 10,000 gate, to be half of nothing. He had fought for free – but he was champion of the world.

Not that he should have been, according to the Americans on their return home, where the verdict so sportingly accepted in London had become a robbery. Whether Willie seriously thought so or whether it was a ploy to improve his chance of a rematch, who knows? If the latter, it didn't work. Welsh's manager, Harry Pollok, was keen, believing that a repeat performance on American soil would silence the sceptics. But Freddie held out for the same money Ritchie had received in London and the bout never happened.

The pair did meet again, in a 'No Decision' 10-rounder at Madison Square Garden, but Welsh had barely trained. Knowing that only a knockout would cost him his title, he was happy to keep on the move. Willie was given the nod by the ringside scribes, but, still unable to match the champion's financial demands, was no nearer a title fight.

Ritchie boxed for a further 12 years, but never again contested the belt. He went on to serve as chief inspector for the California State Athletic Commission from 1937 to 1961, dying in 1975 at the age of 84.

8

★★★

EDDIE **MORGAN**	vs.	JOHNNY **KILBANE**

JANUARY 21, 1915	National Athletic Club, Philadelphia

★★★

Merthyr Tydfil is renowned for its boxers. After all, there are statues commemorating no fewer than three of them dotted around the town centre. But Eddie Morgan is something of a forgotten hero.

Eddie Morgan, Merthyr's forgotten fighter

The miner from Morgantown had picked up the Welsh flyweight title and proceeded to establish his wider credentials with a thrilling victory over American Young George Pierce, who had previously drawn with British bantam boss Digger Stanley. But instead of waiting for a crack at Stanley, he opted to try his luck across the Atlantic.

He set his sights on the newly crowned world feather champion, an Irish-American from Cleveland. John Patrick Kilbane had not had an easy start in life: his mother died when he was three and seven years later his father went blind. The skinny youngster grew up on the streets, earning a reputation as a dancer, with ambitions that swung between singing, acting and gymnastics.

But when ageing heavyweight Tom Sharkey - he fought the likes of Jack Johnson and John L. Sullivan, using the purse from the Sullivan fight to lay a new floor in his New York home, made entirely from silver dollars – visited Kilbane's local youth club for an exhibition, the boy was entranced. Boxing took over his life.

He progressed through the ranks until, in California in February 1912, he outpointed Jim Driscoll's old foe, Abe Attell, to take the title. As his followers celebrated, the self-effacing Kilbane and his wife pushed a pram along the beach, planning their baby's future.

A few months later his future Welsh rival landed in New York, claiming the newspaper verdict in his first three fights. His impact was such that potential opponents were keeping their heads down, so manager Jimmy Johnston placed an advert in local papers: "Wanted! A bantamweight or featherweight with enough nerve to step within a 24ft ring with Eddie Morgan."

It was, of course, mainly targetting Kilbane, but the champion was back in Ohio, where his wife was expecting their second child. Morgan gave up waiting and sailed back home.

Two years later Eddie left wartime Britain to try again. Kilbane was still on the throne, although in the 'No Decision' era he, like his contemporaries, was happy to cash in on his position without seriously risking it. His title was similarly protected when he finally stepped into the ring with Morgan at the National Athletic Club in Philadelphia.

Eddie was not the same man who had made such an impact on his first visit, but was still good enough to beat the likes of Pal Moore. And neither man was inhibited

Johnny Kilbane, conqueror of Attell

by the bout's official status as an exhibition. Indeed, it turned out to be one of the best six-round scraps ever seen in the City of Brotherly Love.

Morgan took the fight to Kilbane from the first bell and it was as well that the American was in perfect condition. Had he cut any corners in training, Johnny would have been in serious trouble, with the Welshman fizzing in and out and proving that he packed a decent punch. The Clevelander, too, was landing some heavy shots and Eddie surprised many with his ability to survive them.

The fifth and sixth were at a particularly hot pace, with the American trying to end matters, but finding himself consistently on the receiving end.

The system of "newspaper verdicts", brought in to decide the destination of wagers as much as anything else, was hardly the most reliable. In any contest other than the most one-sided, the local man would get the nod from his hometown scribes, while reporters sending accounts to the visitor's area tended to favour their readers' hero. But there were enough neutral observers voting for Morgan to indicate that he had the better of things.

The champion was in no doubt. Appropriately, considering Johnston's original "wanted" ad, he acknowledged as much in an item he inserted in the Lost and Found section of a Philly broadsheet. "Found, by Johnny Kilbane," it read, "a little fighting machine in the person of Eddie Morgan … He is the first knight of the padded mitts who has made me open wide my speed-throttle in many a moon."

The duo met again three weeks later; this time even a local writer called it a draw. But that was as near as Eddie would come to a world title. A third meeting, four years on, saw the fading Morgan on the deck, with Kilbane this time an undisputed victor, and as the Welshman's decline continued, he could no longer point to bias in the number of verdicts going against him. He hung up his gloves in 1920, but remained in the US.

Johnny, on the other hand, held on to his crown until 1923, when he was stopped in seven rounds by Frenchman Eugène Criqui and promptly retired. He became a referee and was sufficiently respected as a citizen to be elected to the Ohio State Senate in 1941.

Morgan had died four years earlier, just 47, after collapsing in a Philadelphia street during a heatwave. Kilbane lived until 1957, when, at 68, he succumbed to cancer.

9

The little Welshman had already achieved legendary status throughout Britain. His seemingly fragile frame, coupled with an unexpected power of punch, had gained him a devoted following. And he was already acknowledged as a world champion, something that raised a few eyebrows across the Atlantic, where they tended to regard themselves as the only arbiters in such matters.

In an attempt to create a global authority, rather than leaving things in the hands of American promoters and their propagandists in the press, the International Boxing Union was established in Paris in 1911 – and, in fairness, New York and some other US states backed the idea.

The new body's first titleholders at flyweight included Porth's Percy Jones, but it was only when another Rhondda product – Wilde was born at Quakers Yard, in the Merthyr borough, but the family moved to Tylorstown when he was a toddler - succeeded to the throne that the Americans took an interest. They had always considered boxers under eight stone too small to bother with and recognised no weight class below bantam.

Indeed, when Pennsylvania businessman Frank Torreyson asked Cardiff journalist Charles Barnett to recommend a couple of youngsters to sail to

Jimmy Wilde and the Lonsdale Belt

*Johnny Rosner, handicapped
from the start*

the States and appear on his shows, he dismissed the suggested Wilde as too tiny to appeal to his clientèle. Just as well, for Jimmy's sake: the two boys who replaced him were lost with the Titanic.

Four years later, however, tales of the 'Ghost with the Hammer in his Hand' had reached some influential ears in the US. Affronted by the concept of a world title being claimed without their involvement, they searched for someone who could put this upstart in his place. Enter Johnny Rosner.

A product of the New York Jewish fighting tradition, the visitor was said by some to be the US champion, but no such honour existed. Two years younger and two inches shorter than Wilde, he, like his opponent, weighed several pounds inside the fly limit and both mounted the scales fully dressed.

But Johnny began with a handicap: his left eye was bruised from a head clash in sparring and the damage was visible even to those in the back row of a capacity crowd. Despite the obvious target, Jimmy took no early risks, evading Rosner's swings and confining himself to a few feelers with the left. The third round, however, saw the champion whip over a few sharp rights and the fragile skin alongside the American's injury gave way, blood pouring down his cheek.

It ended whatever hopes he might have had. Rosner showed immense courage and durability, although Wilde was rarely troubled, despite a couple of low blows in the seventh which brought Johnny a stern word from referee Eugene Corri.

The affair became painfully one-sided until Jim Lundie, the New Yorker's trainer, jumped through the ropes in the 11th, conceding defeat and saving his man from his own bravery.

Jimmy was fulsome in his praise. "I'd never have believed that any boy so badly handicapped could have fought so pluckily and for so long in such trouble," he said.

The Rosner camp asked for another chance to show what he could do and duly outpointed one of Wilde's sparmates, Porth's Johnny Evans, in the same hall a few weeks later. Further bouts had been lined up for him, but he headed for home to allow his facial damage to recover and never returned to Britain.

Johnny continued to campaign on home ground for a further seven years. He died in 1974, at the age of 79.

10

★★★

FREDDIE	VS.	AD
WELSH		**WOLGAST**

JULY 4, 1916	**Stockyards Stadium, Denver**

★★★

It was two years since Freddie had become world lightweight champion. A man who always insisted that he boxed for money, rather than glory, he had travelled throughout North America, picking up pay cheques without ever seriously risking his crown.

There had been a planned showdown with former ruler Battling Nelson in Cuba, but, in the aftermath of the controversial Jack Johnson-Jess Willard heavyweight clash, the island's government had tried to ban boxing. Although the supreme court threw out their bill, the uncertainty scuppered Freddie's fight and it was back to what were often little more than public exhibitions across Canada and the US.

There were some decent men among the no-hopers in the opposite corner and several of them left with the newspaper verdicts, but nobody came close to knocking out the touring monarch, the only way in which the title could change hands in this 'No Decision' era.

Adolphus Wolgast had already shared the ring with Welsh twice. Their first meeting, a few months after Freddie defeated Willie Ritchie, ended in eight rounds when a tearful Ad, having broken his right arm three sessions earlier, acknowledged the inevitable. The second, in March 1916, saw the Pontypridd man hand out a one-sided beating

Ad Wolgast, 'The Michigan Wildcat'

23

before a 5,000 crowd in Milwaukee, with the ringside hacks all agreed that they had seen a Welsh victory,

The 'Michigan Wildcat' had briefly retired after losing the throne to Ritchie via a disqualification that, unsurprisingly, he considered unfair – indeed, he called it a day repeatedly, only to succumb each time to the desire to right that perceived wrong and reclaim his property. And his rough-edged, all-action style made him a big draw, so Freddie, who had seen a vision of the future when losing a newspaper decision to the fast-rising Benny Leonard in New York, was happy to cash in with a third encounter, especially as a good turnout was guaranteed on the Independence Day holiday in Denver.

It was the first time in two years that Welsh had signed up for a contest as long as 15 rounds. And he knew what he was facing. Wolgast was one of the dirtiest fighters in history: his victory over Nelson involved far more than mere fists in one of the most uncompromising wars ever seen. And the number of disqualifications in his loss column showed where most of the blame lay.

The fans in Colorado were soon to see Ad's street-fighter survival instincts at work. In the second, Welsh landed a right cross which sent Wolgast lurching back to the ropes. His immediate response was to whip in a low right which doubled the champion in half, referee Otto Floto desperately trying to halt the action. Claiming he had not seen the punch, Floto called on the ringside doctors to examine Freddie and they confirmed that there was both bruising and a noticeable dent in the Welshman's protector.

But, because the medics, naturally, could not testify as to how badly damaged the victim was, the third man ordered the pair to continue. The delay had lasted 19 minutes and many had left the arena, assuming the bout was over. They missed an unsavoury spectacle.

An angry Welsh battered Wolgast from pillar to post, Ad's only answer a series of assaults on Freddie's nether regions. In the 11th his transgressions became so blatant that even the hapless Floto had seen enough, pulling the 'Wildcat' off and raising the hand of his pain-wracked opponent.

It later transpired that there had been a conspiracy to dethrone Freddie, with Wolgast given carte blanche to do what he had to in order to get the necessary knockout. Fortunately for Welsh, the referee – eventually – stood up for law and order.

"Possibly he is getting old and desperate," said Freddie of his ageing rival, "but he certainly is vicious in his style."

Fate had further retribution in store for Wolgast. He spent the rest of his life in and out of mental hospitals until a California gym owner, Jack Doyle, took him in and allowed him to train for a fight "tomorrow". Tomorrow, of course, never came. Ad lived on until 1955, when he died of heart failure. He did not even know he had been champion.

11

★★

FREDDIE		CHARLEY
WELSH	**VS.**	**WHITE**

SEPTEMBER 4, 1916	Ramona Athletic Club Arena, Colorado Springs

★★

When a newspaper asked its readers to nominate Freddie Welsh's next challenger, the vote went overwhelmingly in favour of Charley White. But, despite the fact that the poll was the idea of the champion's manager, Harry Pollok, it was more than a year before the Chicago fighter had his chance.

The pair were well known to each other. After all, they had met three times already in 'No Decision' 10-rounders since Welsh had claimed the title. Two were in Milwaukee, where the newspapermen each time sided with Freddie, but the scribes voted for White when they collided again in New York.

Having survived the foul-fest with Ad Wolgast, Welsh surprised those who thought him on the slippery slope when he gained revenge over the highly touted Benny Leonard. Under pressure to put his belt on the line in a jurisdiction which allowed proper verdicts, he agreed to face White at 6,000 feet above sea level in Colorado Springs.

Charley was actually a Scouser, having been born Charles Anchowitz in Liverpool, though his Russian-Jewish parents took the family to America when the boy was just seven. Six years later he went down with tuberculosis and was sent to a gym to build up his strength.

Despite his skinny frame, he showed natural boxing ability, but only realised that he had power in his fists after a row with a burly lorry driver, whose vehicle had splashed mud on his new trousers. The outraged youngster yelled a

Charley White, a challenger by public demand

protest, the driver pulled up and came over to sort him out – and Charley flattened him with one punch.

His left hook, in particular, became feared throughout the sport, but Charley lacked a fighting brain, which had already cost him one opportunity to capture the lightweight crown.

Even in bouts where no formal decision could be given, a title would change hands if the challenger managed to knock the holder out. Facing Willie Ritchie, White had his man in all sorts of trouble in the opener, but stood off and allowed him to recover. History repeated itself against Ritchie's successor.

The fight nearly didn't happen. A railway strike threatened to prevent out-of-town fans attending, but was called off just in time. Then, an hour and a half before the scheduled start, a stand collapsed, with its 400 occupants crashing to the ground. One man died, two women broke their backs and more than 150 other people were badly hurt. To help the emergency services deal with the casualties, it was decided not to admit any further ticket-holders, with at least 2,000 refused entry. But the fight still went ahead on schedule.

Although White won the toss, choosing the corner with the sun behind him, Freddie began the opener by manoeuvring his foe to the other side, a position he was rarely able to change. Blood soon mingled with the perspiration on Charley's face when an old cut on his nose was reopened as Freddie repeatedly landed his left lead, rarely bothering to employ the right at all.

The only moment of concern for Welsh's backers came in the 13th, when Charley finally found the target with his renowned left hook. But, as against Ritchie, he was slow to realise Freddie was hurt, allowing the champion to regain control for the rest of the 20 rounds. Few knowledgeable observers disagreed with referee Billy Roche's decision; even White's own pet official, fellow Chicagoan Ed Smith, watching from ringside, supported his colleague's view that Welsh had clearly won.

Some of those whose wagers had gone south were less sanguine about the outcome. Scores of cushions were hurled in the direction of the ring and Roche had to be rushed to a waiting car, which sped off, chased by the angry mob. The referee later insisted that the rioters were linked to an alleged plot – similar to that surrounding the Wolgast bout – to ensure that the title changed hands, but an investigation, predictably, got nowhere.

For White it was the last real shot at glory. He continued his career until 1923, once flooring an overweight Leonard, only to be dropped five times himself and knocked out in the ninth. After losing his money in the Depression, he made a disastrous one-fight comeback in 1930, but then moved to Hollywood and earned a decent living teaching film stars to box.

There was no happy ending, however. He subsided into the fog of Alzheimer's and his wife, after he had chased after her with a knife, had him committed to a psychiatric ward, where he died in 1959, aged 68.

12

★★

JIMMY **WILDE**	VS.	YOUNG **ZULU KID**
DECEMBER 18, 1916		**Holborn Stadium, London**

★★

The comprehensive victory over Johnny Rosner had convinced most Americans that Jimmy Wilde was a bit special. But it did not stop them hunting for someone to beat him.

The Welshman had domestic foes to deal with, gaining revenge over former conqueror Tancy Lee and then seeing off veteran Londoner Johnny Hughes, before the next transatlantic challenger hove into view. And this time even the insular US media declared themselves willing to recognise the match as deciding the top flyweight in the world.

Young Zulu Kid was an unlikely nom de guerre for someone born in Italy as Giuseppe di Melfi. Indeed, in those racially conscious times it was a strange name for any white boxer to choose and, several months after the Wilde fight, one American newspaper thought it necessary to publish a short article with the headline, "Young Zulu Kid is not Colored Boy".

His family migrated to Brooklyn when Giuseppe was three and as a youngster he earned a crust selling papers, earning him the nickname 'The Fighting Newsboy'. Just 4ft 11in, the muscular midget began boxing as a teenager and faced Rosner numerous times in the 'No Decision' bouts then the rule in New York; on those occasions when the verdict of watching newspapermen was recorded, Rosner was seen as the better man. The Kid brushed aside such trivia and headed for London claiming he was the true champion.

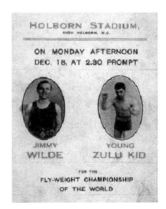

He certainly impressed Tommy Noble, a sparring partner at Brighton in the lead-up to the visitor's meeting with Wilde. Bermondsey boy Noble, halted by Jimmy six weeks earlier, forecast in a letter to *Boxing* that the Kid would spring an upset when they met in the first show

"Young Zulu Kid is not Colored Boy"

at the former Holborn Theatre, now said to be the best-appointed hall in the country. Others were unconvinced, many observers forecasting a swift Welsh victory; they finished red-faced, while a host of Wilde fans had lighter wallets after putting their money where the pundits' mouths were.

The Kid scaled 7st 12½ lb (110½ lb), presumably heavier than the champion, who, as usual, stepped on the scales fully clad. But once the pair came together in the ring for the afternoon start, Wilde towered over the tiny New Yorker, even if his pipe-stem legs were hardly comparable to his rival's solid limbs.

Not that the height difference worried Giuseppe – after all, he was used to it. He turned it to his advantage, becoming even shorter as he bent his knees to duck under Wilde's punches. The manoeuvre did not merely frustrate the 'Tylorstown Terror', it frequently resulted in his occasionally suspect knuckles making worrying contact with solid bone instead of yielding flesh.

The Kid was also able to work his way in close and score to the body, with Jimmy taking some time to figure out this unusual problem. He found an answer in the uppercut and one such blow late in the second, followed by a right cross, staggered the American, who looked on the verge of collapse. Yet it took another three rights before he subsided to the canvas and the bell came to his rescue.

Showing remarkable powers of recovery, the Kid was back on his toes by the fourth, only to be wobbled again in the sixth. The champion was clearly on top, but Giuseppe still appeared to hurt him with left hooks in the seventh and ninth.

It was not something that happened often, but a wounded Wilde was a dangerous animal. His left constantly reached its target in the 10th, the steady punishment having its effect on the already tiring American. Scenting blood, Jimmy stormed out for Round 11 and unleashed a two-fisted onslaught as the Kid tried to cover up in his own corner. It took a dozen blows before the brave New Yorker finally crumpled, just as manager Joe Sarno threw in the towel.

The pair met again three years later when Wilde toured North America, boxing a 10-round No Decision bout in Canada; Jimmy floored his man early and won the votes of the watching pressmen. As referees' decisions were reintroduced, the Kid found himself on the wrong end of them. When he finally retired in 1928, he had not won a fight for eight years.

Wilde on guard as the Kid moves in

13

★★

FREDDIE
WELSH

vs.

BENNY
LEONARD

| **MAY 28, 1917** | **Manhattan Casino, New York** |

★★

The world lightweight champion had a stalker – and this one had an entourage. For several years a young New Yorker had been proclaiming himself the inevitable successor to Freddie Welsh. And there were newsrooms full of scribes ready to agree.

Benjamin Leiner was one of those Jewish kids who had to learn to scrap in order to survive the ethnic street-fighting of Manhattan's East Village. He sorted out the local yobs to such effect that, at just 11, he became known as 'The King of Eighth Street'. Not that his devoutly religious mother joined in the praise.

To avoid her recriminations when he eventually turned pro, he would go to bed early on fight nights before sneaking out under cover of darkness; in the mornings, he would tell her he was heading off to look for a job and then work out in a local park. But fear of maternal wrath was not behind the change in his name.

Before his first bout, Benny was so nervous that he was only able to mumble a reply when the MC asked what he was called. The man misheard Leiner and proceeded to announce him as 'Benny Leonard'. It was an error that resonated through history.

His mother's disapproval did, however, influence his style. He endeavoured to win through sheer science, avoiding punishment – and the resultant

Benny Leonard lived and died in the ring

Welsh (left) and Leonard before the storm

bruises – as much as possible. When the plan failed and he returned home one night with a black eye and $20 in cash, Mama wept. But his father, who slaved all week in a garment factory for the same amount, quietly urged him to keep fighting.

It proved good advice as Benny kept busy, picking up valuable experience as well as earning enough to move his family to better accommodation in Jewish Harlem. He was swiftly moving through the lightweight ranks and a dramatic knockout of the 'Milwaukee Marvel', Richie Mitchell, in his own home city, left Leonard hammering on Freddie Welsh's door.

They first came together at Madison Square Garden in 1915, Benny's dazzling skills earning the newspaper verdict, but the reporters saw things the other way in a rematch in Brooklyn, after the over-confident Leonard found himself outfoxed by the wily Welshman. Yet he was still widely regarded as the greatest threat to the title and, amid growing criticism of his apparent unwillingness to face serious opposition, Freddie finally agreed a third meeting.

He was hardly in the best of form going in, following three defeats in quick succession, the most recent to featherweight king Johnny Kilbane. The challenger, on the other hand, had halted his last four rivals. Not that it seemed to dent Welsh's confidence, judging by his comment when referee Billy McPartland explained the new rule insisting a boxer retreated to a neutral corner following a knockdown.

"Do you mean I've got to go to a neutral corner *every* time I knock him down," he inquired. But it was Benny who had to put the new regulation into effect.

New York still adhered to the 'No Decision' rule and Welsh was certain Leonard, even if he had the better of matters, would not achieve the stoppage necessary for the crown to change hands. But Leonard had rethought his strategy after his head-hunting tactic had failed in their second engagement; this time he went for the body, reasoning that Welsh, a decade older, would weaken.

By the start of the ninth Freddie's hands were coming down to protect his battered midriff. Hardly had the bell's echo died than Leonard took advantage of the gap in the champion's defence and whipped over a right to the temple. Welsh staggered and Benny saw his opportunity: he drove his tiring target to the ropes and a one-two sent the holder to the deck, only to bounce up before a count could commence.

A follow-up assault floored him a second time. And although he clambered to his feet again, Freddie was exhausted. He became entangled in the ropes as he tried to evade Leonard's onslaught and the referee had to step between them and release the champion's trapped left arm. When the count reached four, Welsh staggered across the ring and collapsed over the top rope. It was all over.

Freddie, the supposed inspiration for The Great Gatsby

Benny, the first native New Yorker to win a world title, was to reign for nearly eight years. He was still the undefeated champion when he announced his retirement in 1925, yielding to the prayers of his seriously ill mother. The Wall Street Crash four years later wrecked his finances, prompting a comeback at welterweight: he was unbeaten for 20 contests, but when Jimmy McLarnin destroyed him in six rounds, the 'Ghetto Wizard' took the hint and quit for good.

He later became a referee and was handling a bout at Manhattan's legendary St Nick's Arena in 1947, when he suffered a fatal heart attack, dying, as he had lived, in the ring.

For Welsh, although there were a handful of fights against no-hopers, the loss of his title was effectively the end. He bought a property in New Jersey, which he converted into a health farm, but, despite the patronage of world heavyweight king Jack Dempsey, it became a financial millstone and was sold at a huge loss.

Freddie, once fêted by film stars and writers, slid down the social ladder, his descent lubricated by a fondness for the drink. He died alone in a cheap lodging-house at the age of 41.

14

LLEW EDWARDS

vs.

HARRY STONE

SEPTEMBER 29, 1917	Brisbane Stadium

Llew Edwards, champion in two countries

Hiram Llewellyn Edwards had been so averse to fisticuffs when growing up on a Shropshire farm that he let his kid brother settle his arguments for him. But after he moved south to work in the Rhondda coalfield, pacifism was no longer an option.

An argument below ground led to him being badly beaten up by a heavier man who held his head with one arm while punching him with the other. Llew's workmates insisted he had to challenge his tormentor to a rematch in the ring, where such illegality would not be allowed. The reluctant Edwards was finally persuaded – and sparked his rival with one blow.

When he realised his unsuspected talent could be converted into cash, there was no holding Llew. He soon built a reputation across the land and, after barely two years as a pro, won the British featherweight crown, dethroning former world bantam king Owen Moran, whose increasing desperation drove him to employ some of the more dubious tactics he had learned while campaigning in the States. After straying below the belt once too often, Moran was disqualified and Edwards was the proud owner of a Lonsdale Belt.

Yet that was to be his last contest in front of a British crowd, apart from one on a brief visit home five years later. Llew and trainer George Baillieu

Brisbane Stadium, the mecca of Queensland fight fans

boarded the *Orontes* to undertake a multi-fight contract in Australia and liked it so much they decided to stay.

He made quite an impact, flooring national titleholder Jimmy Hill eight times on the way to winning the dormant Empire honour. A year later and now a lightweight, he added the championship of his adopted land with victory over Herbie McCoy, repeating the feat in his first defence.

But there had been one opponent he had never been able to overcome since arriving Down Under – and he, too, was an immigrant, this time from the US. Harry Stone was a Jewish New Yorker, formerly (and formally) known as Harry Siegstein, who used to sell newspapers at the Bronx Zoo. He arrived in Australia in 1913 with a useful CV which included a draw against Abe Attell.

Dubbed 'Hop Harry' for his habit of jumping in with his left lead and bouncing back out before a counter could arrive, the eccentric American frequently entered the ring wearing a skull cap and puffing on a large cigar. It seemed to have little effect on his fighting ability and he had already beaten Llew twice and drawn with

'Hop Harry' Stone

him once by the time they were matched at the Brisbane Stadium, with the national belt at stake.

There was one important difference from their previous meetings - referee Mike Marre would not allow Stone to perform one of his many little tricks. He was adept at trapping opponents' gloves beneath his arms, arching his back to pull them off-balance and then landing a few shots before they regained control. Marre quickly broke up clinches and insisted on proper action. "That suited me," recalled Edwards. "It didn't suit Stone – and that's how I got the points decision."

After 20 "strenuously contested" rounds, Marre's verdict "met with a mixed reception"; Harry later claimed that Llew had confessed it had been a lucky break for him. Whatever he might have conceded at the time, Edwards certainly didn't see it like that in retrospect!

It was to be his only success against 'Hop Harry'. Having taken over Llew's title when the fading Welshman was on an unsuccessful trip to the US, Stone outscored him in a defence in Sydney. And it was the New Yorker who ended Edwards's glittering career.

Llew was, by this time, almost blind and could barely see across the ring. It was all too easy for Harry, who eventually refused to keep hitting the man he called "the gamest little fighter who ever donned a boxing glove". When the referee hesitated, Baillieu took the hint and threw in the towel. Llew remained in Australia, dying there in 1965 at the age of 72.

Stone, although three years older than his rival, boxed on until 1929 and was never beaten inside the distance. He also stayed Down Under, where he died in 1950, aged 61. Edwards paid due tribute to "the hardest man I ever encountered".

15

JIMMY

WILDE

VS.

PAL

MOORE

| JULY 17, 1919 | Olympia, London |

I t was the opportunity Jimmy Wilde had been clamouring for, the chance to correct an injustice. But this time it was the American visitor who felt hard done by.

Wilde had boxed only sporadically since achieving worldwide recognition as champion, before the authorities decided to celebrate the end of World War I with an inter-services tournament at the Albert Hall, entering Jimmy at bantamweight.

In three-round contests, he saw off New Yorker Joe Lynch (back in civvy street, he was to repeat the success over 15 a few months later) and Australian Digger Evans to set up a final against a sailor from Memphis, Pal Moore.

Thomas Wilson Moore first laced up the gloves after joining the Navy and had soon established himself as a top-level operator, including victories over Young Zulu Kid. He considered himself the world bantam champion, having beaten a previous claimant, Hungarian-born Minnesotan Johnny Ertle, and was flown in especially from Great Lakes, Illinois, where he had been serving as a boxing instructor.

No mug, therefore. But there were few

Pal Moore

Moore lands with the inside of the glove, a failing that cost him dearly

present who thought the American deserved the decision handed him by the three inexperienced military men on judging duty. The crowd erupted in fury and an all-out brawl between Tommies and GIs looked inevitable until the British team's trainer, Sergeant-Instructor Jim Driscoll, was ordered to climb into the ring and tell the mob that he accepted the decision.

The "defeat" rankled with Wilde and he pleaded for a chance to put the record straight. Finally, theatre impresario C.B. Cochran was prevailed upon to promote the 20-round rematch, involving the biggest purse of either man's career: the winner would get £3,000, the loser £2,000 – and there would be a £1,000 sidestake to sweeten the pot.

The Welshman's build-up had been hit by food poisoning from a fish supper, but he had rejected suggestions that he should pull out and appeared fit enough on the night. Both were announced as within the contracted 8st 4lb (116lb), but, unusually, Jimmy agreed to strip for an actual pre-fight weigh-in which revealed him to be 7st 7½lb (105½lb). Pal was said to scale 8st 3lb (115lb).

Moore, like Wilde, boxed with hands low, but his crouch and fleetness of foot made him difficult to catch cleanly. Nevertheless, Jimmy landed frequently enough and seemed to hurt the visitor in the second, only for hesitancy to rob him of the possibility of an early ending.

Wilde's left spent much time in close contact with Pal's features, while the American's principal failing was already obvious. Many of his punches were thrown with an open glove, a custom which would go unremarked in home rings, but offended British sensibilities and produced several lectures from referee Eugene Corri.

Moore launched an attack after the bell to end the ninth, having apparently failed to hear the gong, and there were shouts for a disqualification, but Mr Corri murmured to Wilde, "I can't caution him, Jimmy. General Pershing is here – it would look so bad!"

The leader of the US Expeditionary Forces, seated alongside the Prince of Wales at ringside, saw his countryman step up the pace after halfway, efforts which prompted his cornermen to spray him with increasing amounts of water each interval. Wilde's lip was cut in the 14th, although he was still happy to engage in some thrilling toe-to-toe exchanges. One such, in the 16th, ended with Jimmy's nose streaming blood, its owner complaining that Pal's head had caused the damage. Mr Corri ignored the claim.

Wilde suffered a rather torrid time in that round and the next, but found enough in the tank to stage a high-octane finish, although disconcerted in the last session when liniment on Moore's body found its way into the Welshman's eyes.

The roar at the final bell indicated the crowd's view. Mr Corri concurred, immediately pointing to Wilde before the ring was invaded by the winner's jubilant backers. The Moore corner looked shocked, although they received the verdict sportingly.

Afterwards, Pal said he had thought his open-palm punches were counting, although, given that he had repeatedly been told by the referee to close his glove – and, indeed, had done so for a period following each admonition – his confusion seemed strange.

But, with perhaps a tinge of sarcasm, the American acknowledged the correctness of the decision. "It's a boxer's business to satisfy the public," he said, "and there isn't a doubt that most of the crowd thought Jimmy was winning all the way. I must have been well beaten – I can't pretend that my opinion ought to outweigh those of 16,000 other judges."

Wilde admitted remembering little for several minutes after the head clash that split his nose, conceding that Moore had power. "He can hurt with some of his slaps," said Jimmy. "He's a strong, game fighter, defends himself well and isn't easy to land on. He might be a world-beater if he could punch properly."

Moore, inevitably, called for a third meeting, but it was not forthcoming. He returned to London later in the year, halting Frenchman Eugène Criqui, and continued boxing at home until 1930. He died in 1953 and was elected to the Hall of Fame in 2011.

16

This was a match that took time in the making. When the little Welsh maestro visited the US in 1920, one name kept cropping up as a potential opponent: the world bantamweight king from New Orleans, Pete Herman. But nothing materialised and Jimmy Wilde returned home from a lucrative, but exhausting tour thinking of retirement.

Any such plans were put on the back burner when he heard that Herman, who had previously reached an agreement with London promoter Charles Cochran only to change his mind, was now willing to travel, persuaded by a generous offer from West End actor Rube Welch.

Pete Herman

Real name Peter Gulotta, with Sicilian-born parents, he was just 12, shining shoes in a barber's shop, when he came across a copy of *The Police Gazette*, which carried reports on the fight game. Enchanted by the stories and their accompanying pictures, Pete began practising moves in front of the shop's full-length mirrors, something which did not impress his employer. But a dream had been born.

Soon he was making his name in local rings, with future Wilde foe Johnny Rosner an early victim, earning a shot at world bantam ruler Kid Williams, in which Herman dominated but was awarded no more than a draw after the 20 rounds; as part of the deal to get him to New Orleans, Williams had been allowed to choose his own referee. But a cunning plan was taking shape in Southern minds.

Williams was tempted back to the 'Big Easy', and the home camp insisted that the same arbiter, Billy Rocap, should again be the third man. They calculated that the Philadelphia official would realise that his reputation would not survive a repeat performance. It worked a treat. Pete put the Kid down twice and this time Rocap gave him the decision – and the title, which he held for three years.

He lost it to former Wilde victim Joe Lynch weeks before setting sail for Britain – suspicions that it was a deliberate move to avoid the risk of the crown leaving American hands were enhanced when Herman regained it in a rematch after returning home – so there was only pride at stake when he and Jimmy came face to face at the Albert Hall, even though the bout was over the championship distance, despite the Welshman's preference for 15 rounds.

There were to be other hitches before the first bell rang. Fans in the cheap seats discovered that their view was masked by a canopy covering the lights needed for filming, while there was a further blow when American heavyweight Battling Levinsky claimed he had damaged an elbow and pulled out of the chief support against Bombardier Billy Wells.

Backstage there were other bones of contention. Wilde had expected both men to weigh in at fight-time, but Herman had done so at 2 p.m., brandishing a contract to that effect, and then disappeared for a late lunch. There would now be about a stone and a half – 21 pounds in US terms – between them and manager Teddy Lewis was among several urging Jimmy not to fight. Despite his anger at being manipulated, Wilde insisted he would go ahead – after all, his illustrious admirer, the Prince of Wales, was at ringside.

Nevertheless, the MC was instructed to tell the gathering of the changed circumstances and announce that all bets should be null and void. It was a signal that even the normally super-confident Jimmy feared the worst.

Whether the result of declining ambition, a lack of fitness or simply resignation following the pre-fight shenanigans, from the start it was clear to those present that they were not looking at the Wilde of old. His left was without snap, his movement lacked energy, he looked even more sickly than usual. As early as the second, Herman rocked him with a right to the jaw, but failed to realise the stunning effect of the punch and stood off.

Jimmy gradually began to find a semblance of the old rhythm, but without ever convincing. He won his share of the middle rounds and, had the contest been restricted to 15 rounds, as the Welshman had wished, he

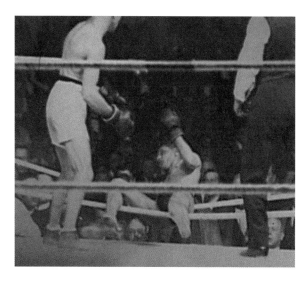

Just too big - Herman knocks Wilde through the ropes

might have had a claim to the decision; indeed, referee Jack Smith confessed later that he had had him ahead. But he was tiring – he had not seen action for seven months and there were suggestions that his preparation had been less than thorough – and Pete looked as strong as when he started.

Wilde had also injured his right hand and the left alone was not sufficient to keep the visitor at bay. In the 17th, Herman drove Jimmy back before unleashing a right that sent him through the ropes to strike his head on the ring apron. Twice more he was floored, twice more he somehow pulled himself up, but on the third occasion Mr Smith grabbed him around the waist and half-carried him to his corner, whispering, "I've got to pick you up, Jimmy, because you don't know the way to stay down."

Herman headed home and reclaimed his property from Lynch, but lost it two months later to Johnny Buff. By this time Pete could see nothing out of his right eye and the left was heading the same way. He had another half-dozen fights before accepting the inevitable. He was soon completely blind, but still ran a club in the famous French Quarter of his home city, dying in 1973 at the age of 77.

Wilde, chastened by the realisation of how little he had left, announced that he would fight no more. But, like so many boxers before and since, temptation would come knocking on his door.

17

★★★

JOHNNY
BASHAM

VS.

MIKE
McTIGUE

| OCTOBER 25, 1922 | Drill Hall, Sheffield |

★★★

F ew men can have had a more appropriate name for their choice of profession. And John Michael Basham proved he could live up to it. The soldier from Newport did, indeed, bash 'em more often than he was bashed.

But those times were in the past. Behind him were the British, European and Empire welterweight titles, lost gloriously, but decisively in the first of three unsuccessful collisions with the immortal Ted 'Kid' Lewis. Gone, too, the British and European middle crowns, also snatched away by the fearsome fists of the 'Smashing, Dashing, Crashing Kid'.

It was perhaps a bit late in the day to take on one of the world's best at light-heavyweight. Raised in County Clare, the son of a stonemason, Michael Francis McTigue joined the exodus to New York, where he was introduced to boxing by his stockyard boss, impressed by the way the Irishman

Johnny Basham had the name for the job

MIKE McTIGUE "The Cyclonic Celt"
WHO MADE PUGILISTIC HISTORY OVER NIGHT

had dealt with an argumentative trucker.

A late starter in the game, McTigue had to learn on the job, with inevitable setbacks early on. But by the time he returned to Europe in 1922 he had enjoyed two spells as Canadian middleweight champion, during an 18-month spell north of the border.

With Ireland in turmoil, Mike headed for Sheffield, where he had family. His target was Lewis, but the 'Kid' insisted he first prove himself on this side of the Atlantic. Hence the meeting with Basham.

Johnny had joined the Royal Welsh Fusiliers in 1912 and, as usual, prepared at the regiment's Wrexham headquarters. At least, that was the plan. But just three weeks before the bout that could have brought new light to a fading star, Basham was laughing and joking with friends in London. Perhaps he was over-confident, perhaps he knew, within himself, that no amount of training would have made much difference.

The post-fight talk was not of Basham's decline, but full of excited admiration for the recent arrival. "McTigue is a Marvel" read a cross-head in *Boxing*'s account, summing up its reporter's awe at the Irishman's display.

Basham was able to demonstrate his own skilful boxing in the opener, as his fellow-Celt eased into the bout, but Mike was already seen to be lining up the right hand that had brought him so many quick victories in the States. The visitor took the initiative in the second, although Johnny landed a right cross which gave him pause for thought.

Basham's attempts to reinforce that single success were thwarted by a left to the body and a right hook and the Welshman then contented himself with jabbing from long range. They were scoring punches, but lacked venom and McTigue waited patiently for his opportunity.

It came early in the third. Johnny was flicking out the left, with his opponent replying in kind, but keeping his powerful right under wraps. Then came the opening: for a split second, Basham's guard was lowered. McTigue took one pace forward, fired in a left to the body and brought over a right which travelled no more than 18 inches. Johnny dropped to the floor, already unconscious, remaining motionless throughout referee Jack Smith's count.

For Basham, retirement beckoned. There were two attempts at a comeback: two years later, he was outpointed by cross-town rival Jerry Shea, while a rash return in 1929 saw the 39-year-old wiped out yet again by nemesis Lewis. Having taken an easy come, easy go attitude to money, Johnny struggled in civvy street. There were summers in the booths, a spell as a London fireman which ended when a training accident put him in hospital, a flirtation with the stage and a period pulling pints in a friend's pub in County Durham. None lasted long.

His later years, back in his home town, were spent in poverty, although those "laughing blue eyes" were still twinkling and he claimed he was happy. But his health was failing and he died of a heart attack in 1947, just eight days before a tournament intended to provide him with a pension.

For McTigue, in contrast, victory over Basham moved him closer to glory. With the world light-heavy king, Battling Siki, based in Europe, a couple more victories in England created sufficient stir to prompt talk of a crack at the crown. With Africa's first world champion refused entry to Britain as a supposed "undesirable", a clash in Dublin was mooted.

Siki, with few other options, agreed to the deal. Perhaps he didn't realise that he was taking on an Irishman on St Patrick's Day in the middle of the Troubles. There were gunshots heard in the streets and a bomb went off outside the La Scala theatre. Inside, McTigue won on points to become the first Irishman to win a world title on home soil.

Benefiting from the 'No Decision' rule, McTigue wore the belt for two years and continued to box for another five. But, even though he had looked after his money, drink and a street attack saw him end his days in a psychiatric institution, where he died in 1966, at the age of 73.

18

★★★

JIMMY		PANCHO
WILDE	VS.	**VILLA**

JUNE 18, 1923	Polo Grounds, New York

★★★

Even fighters who have done well out of the game can be tempted to return if the money is right. Jimmy Wilde was fully aware that the passage of time had eroded many of his wondrous skills, while also realising that he no longer possessed the driving ambition necessary to dedicate himself to the tedium of training. When he called it a day, following his demolition by Pete Herman, he intended his decision to be final.

'Ring' honours Villa on cover

But that loss, up at bantam, had not affected his status in the flyweight division. Nobody had stepped up to take his place; certainly, as far as the Americans were concerned, the 'Tylorstown Terror' was still the champion of the world.

And they felt that they had, in 1920 Olympic gold medallist Frankie Genaro, a man who could claim the crown for the US. To gain full recognition, they needed him to beat Wilde, even if the Welshman had retired. So they dangled a cheque for £8,000 in front of Jimmy, a massive sum for a single fight. When that figure was raised to £13,000, it could no longer be ignored, something with which wife Lisbeth agreed.

But there was an unexpected hitch. Genaro wanted too much money. Up stepped a Filipino named Pancho Villa. Born Francisco Villaruel Guilledo, he was using his new name before a Mexican revolutionary made it famous; 'Pancho'

Wilde arrives in New York

is the diminutive of Francisco, while Villa was the surname of his adoptive father.

He moved from his native Iloilo to Manila, sleeping on the stone floors of empty buildings as he learned his craft in the ring. Ironically, one of those who passed on a few hints to the youngster was a Welshman, former British feather king Llew Edwards, on a visit to the islands from his new home in Australia.

Manager Frank Churchill took Villa to New York in 1922 and he was soon recognised as American fly champion – the Philippines were then a US colony - after flooring and outscoring future bantam boss Johnny Buff. He was deposed by Genaro, but even Frankie admitted that the colourful Oriental was the man the public loved. No wonder the promoters were happy to call him up as a stand-in for the demanding ex-Olympian!

More than 40,000 (never before had two flyweights attracted such a crowd) flocked to the Polo Grounds, but they were not to watch an even contest. It was almost two and a half years since the champion had last seen action - and that was a stoppage loss. He was now 31, while Villa was 10 years younger, but had nevertheless picked up a wealth of experience.

For the challenger, the fight was won with the first punch, a left to the

The pair pose before Jimmy's last fight

body. Wilde clinched and Pancho felt his arm being grabbed tightly, as if Jimmy was afraid to let go. Villa claimed that from then on he knew he would prevail.

For the Welshman and his followers, it was decided by a right thrown by the Filipino after the bell to end the second. Jimmy had already dropped his hands and the unexpected blow sent him face-first to the deck. Cornerman Benny Williams dragged him to his stool and managed to revive him enough to send him back out for five more rounds, none of which he would remember.

The slaughter ended in the seventh. A succession of rights beat Wilde to the canvas and the ageing legend was no longer able to beat the count. In fact, he was unconscious for several hours, Lisbeth sure her man was dying. When he finally came round, it took three weeks' recuperation in a cottage loaned them by bantamweight Frankie Burns before Jimmy was fully in command of his senses.

Villa had become Asia's first world champion. But he was not to enjoy his success for long. He ignored badly infected teeth to go through with a non-title fight, following it with a week-long party, and had to be rushed to a San Francisco hospital for emergency surgery. While under the anaesthetic he lapsed into a coma, dying the following day. He was just 23.

Wilde turned his attention to journalism, also guiding the brief career of son David, while serving as founder-president of the short-lived National Union of Boxers. He was badly hurt in an unprovoked attack by a 40-year-old man at Cardiff's Queen Street station, the effects of which saw him live out his final years in a psychiatric hospital. The greatest boxer Wales ever produced died in 1969, at the age of 76.

19

★★

FRANK
VS.
LOU

MOODY   BOGASH

| MAY 19, 1924 | State Street Arena, Bridgeport |

★★

I t all began with an argument at a Pontypridd school. Young Frank Moody, the oldest of 13 children, fell out with a classmate and it came to blows. Frank's punch proved the more effective: it knocked its hapless recipient into the nearby canal.

Father George, a former mountain fighter, heard what had happened and, realising his son's potential, promptly began regular lessons. They paid off. After turning pro at 13, young Frank stormed through the ranks to become the first Welshman to win British titles at two weights, although those triumphs came late in his career.

The Welsh middleweight crown was his while still a teenager, however, and four years later came the chance to seek fame and fortune across the Atlantic. He was soon to discover that things were a bit different in the States.

When Moody faced Joe Jackson before a crowd of emigrant Welsh miners in Wilkes-Barre, Pennsylvania, matchmaker Al Dewey became so frustrated by the referee's reluctance to stop Jackson holding that he climbed into the ring, evicted the

Frank Moody (right) and Francis Rossi spar in the yard of Moody's Pontypridd home - both youngsters were to box in the US

Lou Bogash

errant official and took over himself. When he then came to separate the pair and pushed Joe back, that worthy took umbrage and punched him. Dewey, a former pro, replied in kind and the police had to intervene and abandon the show.

At least there were no such shenanigans when Frank took on Lou Bogash in Connecticut. Born Luigi Boccasio at Faeto, in Southern Italy, the 'Blond Italian' had grown up on the north side of Bridgeport and became state lightweight king at the tender age of 17.

He grew through the weight divisions and was an established middleweight by the time he met Moody for the first time, in Boston, where Bogash was given the nod after 10 close rounds. Three months later they collided again and perhaps Lou was over-confident after their first encounter. Certainly, he was to pay for it.

Frank had just made a trip home to see the family and rest the hands that had been giving him problems. Fresh off the boat, he arrived at Bridgeport three days before the bout and was given an encouraging welcome by the town's British community at a special public workout. Many expats joined the 2,500 crowd at the newly-built arena, but most were there to cheer on their local hero.

Bogash was a useful body-puncher and a renowned spoiler, but his principal attribute was durability. He was inordinately proud of his iron jaw, having never been floored in a record that already consisted of 175 bouts. Moody, boosted by his newly healed hands, was determined that would change.

He stormed out from the first bell, launching a two-fisted onslaught which culminated in a solid right to that granite chin. Bogash staggered, but Frank was the man in real trouble: a searing pain up his arm told him that his thumb was broken. With 12 rounds to go, he would have to face one of the world's toughest middles with only one serviceable fist.

That was to be enough. The Welshman kept the left in Lou's face, occasionally throwing rights to the stomach to conceal the damage from his foe, but there was little between them when they reached the 11th round. Then the American's bravado took over. He suddenly dropped his hands, thrust his chin out and invited Moody to hit it.

Maybe he had been expecting the right and was caught by surprise when Frank hurled a half-hook, half-uppercut with his left. Maybe he simply underestimated his rival's power. Whatever, the supposedly indestructible Bogash was stunned and Moody, his injury forgotten, piled in two-handed. Lou slumped back on the ropes until Frank stepped back, allowing room for his victim to pitch forward to the boards.

He pulled himself upright at seven, but was unable to hold off another Moody assault. Once again, as soon as Frank moved away, Bogash crashed on to his face, out to the world, and his brother, Patsy, joined the referee to drag him to his stool.

The outcome was greeted with stony silence by the Bridgeport crowd, although the mayor did call in at Moody's hotel the following day. It was not, however, to congratulate the Welshman, but to demand compensation for his straw hat, soaked each time manager Billy Ames welcomed his charge back to the corner with a spongeful of water. Billy advised him to take an umbrella next time he sat at ringside!

Bogash learned his lesson. He boxed on for another seven years, but never again did a referee count over him. He later became a referee – as did his son, Lou, Jr – and died at the age of 77, still remembered as a legend of New England boxing.

20

★★

FRANK
MOODY

VS.

HARRY
GREB

JUNE 16, 1924	Brassco Park, Waterbury

★★

Not for nothing was Harry Greb known as the world's dirtiest fighter. Many an opponent could testify to his tendency to improvise on the occasions when legitimate tactics were not getting the job done. And, allied to a genuine talent and a decent punch, his lack of scruples made the 'Pittsburgh Windmill' a difficult man to handle.

After all, he gave future heavyweight king Gene Tunney the only loss on his record, despite conceding 12lb on the scales. Sure, Tunney was to gain his revenge, but Harry earned the right to be considered among the game's greats. And, despite Greb's reputation in and out of the ring – the polar opposite to that of the intellectual and urbane Tunney – Gene was a pall-bearer at his old foe's funeral.

Harry Greb, the world's dirtiest fighter?

Harry had beaten world-class men in the top three weight divisions and was at one time seriously considered as a challenger to Jack Dempsey, but at the time he met Moody he was nine months into a three-year reign as world middleweight champion. He was also blind in one eye, but nobody realised until his death.

His affliction in no way modified his tactics, which were basically to do whatever the referee would permit. And in Jim Galvin, who handled their 10-round non-title encounter, he found an official who was generous in the extreme.

Frank had not had the best of preparation. Manager Billy Ames had ambitiously arranged for him to face No 1 contender Jock Malone and Greb in four days. The Welshman overcame Malone, but then had to travel 200 miles from Boston to take on the world's best middle in a Connecticut baseball park.

Harry's reputation had preceded him, but the gentlemanly Moody, always one to see the best in people, believed he could not be as rough as he had been painted. The opening exchanges were enough to convince Frank the stories had not been exaggerated.

Midway through the opener, Greb butted Moody under the chin and, as Frank's head went back, he felt the laces of the American's gloves being rubbed across his face, while the assault was climaxed by a thumb in his right eye which left the recipient unable to see.

Mr Galvin also appeared to have problems with his vision; at least, he saw nothing wrong, nor with the way Harry would grab Frank's neck with his left while battering the damaged eye with his right. The rest of Greb's dubious arsenal was soon deployed.

Moody and his ambitious manager, Billy Ames

"He gave me the fingertips, the palm, the wrist, the forearm, the elbow and the shoulder and generally one followed the other," recalled Moody, years later. "The way it was done was uncanny and something to marvel at – providing you weren't the target."

A low blow in the fourth sent the Pontypridd fighter to his knees, although he managed to rise at nine, but another body shot dropped him for three. Determined to go down fighting, Moody started hurling both fists and his bravery saw him to the bell.

Billy Ames said he could have one more round, but Frank actually shared the spoils in that session and the manager duly let him out for the sixth. Moody stuck out a left, but Greb evaded it and drilled home a right to the jaw which felled Frank once more. The Welshman waited on one knee, his functioning eye on the third man, and rose at nine, only to find the referee ruling that he had failed to beat the count. A ringside photographer claimed the timer on his camera showed only six seconds had passed, but it was too late to change the outcome.

While Moody needed six weeks to recover from his injuries, Greb was back in the ring after 10 days, seeing off a challenge from Plymouth's Ted Moore, and fought on until 1926, when he was controversially dethroned by Tiger Flowers. Two months later he was dead.

It was all down to vanity. Ladies' man Harry entered hospital for an operation to remove scar tissue and straighten his nose – it was said to be needed following a car crash, but manager Red Mason admitted that was an invention to ward off the mockery that might have followed had it been known he was seeing "a beauty doctor". The surgery was successful, but the following morning his heart failed and medics were unable to save him. He was just 32.

21

Every time he fought, he would read a passage from Psalm 144. He would then carry the Bible into the ring. His devout beliefs earned him the label of 'The Georgia Deacon'. But Theodore Flowers had another nickname. And 'Tiger' gave a better idea of what was likely to happen inside the ropes.

Born in the Deep South, Flowers headed north and found employment in the Philadelphia shipyards. While there, he began boxing, but it was only after returning to Atlanta that he began to take the game seriously and move through the middleweight ranks.

It was a non-title clash with world champion Harry Greb, in which the Pittsburgh fighter for once found himself up against someone as unorthodox

Tiger Flowers

as himself, which brought Tiger to nationwide attention. Greb edged the newspaper verdict, prompting a campaign of calculated outrage from manager Walt Miller which earned Flowers more publicity than if there had been no controversy.

Greb was certainly in no rush to put his belt on the line in a rematch, but Flowers kept winning and his claim for a shot gradually gained momentum. Frank Moody had also been enjoying a run of success and the newspapers branded their meeting an unofficial eliminator, even though it was scheduled for just 10 rounds. At least in Massachusetts there would be an official verdict, rather than having to rely on a consensus of sometimes one-eyed journalists.

Moody's troublesome right hand, injured again in sparring with Scot Tommy Milligan, had forced the Welshman to request a slight delay and, although it was not still not right, the fight was too important for him to risk missing out. When the commission doctor kept pressing and poking the suspect mitt, Frank had to grit his teeth and remain impassive. It worked. He was given the green light.

Mechanics' Hall, Boston

Not that the handicap proved particularly significant. From the start, Tiger was in control. A spidery southpaw, with unusually long arms, he threw his right lead from unexpected angles, landing even when he seemed to be out of range. Moody was so bewildered by the right that when Flowers hurled a left hook late in the opener, it caught him by surprise and he found himself on his rear.

The bell went at the count of two and Frank was fully recovered on the resumption, but still unable to deposit his own punches on the slippery American. "He seemed to be made of grease," said the Pontypridd man, whose rare successes only served to further damage his fragile right.

Moody managed to survive the course, but was frequently in trouble – not least from a badly gashed eyebrow in the ninth - and suspected that Flowers had deliberately eased off. Questioned afterwards, Tiger told him, "I never punish a man more than I can help."

Two months later Flowers faced Greb for the title and earned a close verdict, becoming the first black champion since the flamboyant Jack Johnson had alienated those in high places. It says much for the man's qualities as a human being that he was given the opportunity.

He reigned for just 10 months, however, being controversially outscored by Mickey Walker after a bout in which mobsters were rumoured to have had some influence. And a year later, Tiger was gone: he went into hospital to have some scar tissue removed, there were complications and he never recovered. And just like his old rival, Greb, he was only 32.

Moody, after a mixed last year in North America, headed for home and won British titles at middle and light-heavyweight. He retired in 1936, becoming a publican in Milford Haven and promoting a few shows down west, before returning to his home town, where he died in 1963 at his sister's house in the street where he had been born.

22

★★

GINGER
JONES

VS.

PANAMA
AL BROWN

| SEPTEMBER 21, 1931 | The Pavilion, Mountain Ash |

★★

They were innocent days. Nobody thought it might cause offence when they welcomed the lanky black visitor to the ring with a chorus of *Swanee River*. And, to an extent, it was Panama Al Brown's own fault: he had heard so much about Welsh singing that he had asked that the crowd should sing the national anthem for him. Presumably, in a spirit of fairness, those in attendance wanted to follow up with something the visitor could identify with.

Not that Alfonso Teófilo Brown knew much about "the old plantation". Born in Colón, on Panama's Caribbean coast, he took up boxing, while a clerk in the Canal Zone, after watching American soldiers swapping punches. He proved a natural, his beanpole frame and long arms adding to his innate skill to create a phenomenon.

Within a year of turning pro, he had moved to New York and quickly established himself among the best around. He also spent long periods in Paris, where he supplemented his ring earnings with a stint as a tap dancer in Josephine Baker's stage show and became the lover of the gay writer and film-maker, Jean Cocteau. But it was back in the Big Apple that he outpointed Spaniard Gregorio

Panama Al Brown greets Ginger Jones, watched by referee Bill Allen and promoter Teddy Lewis

Vidal in 1929 to capture the vacant bantamweight title and become Latin America's first world champion.

He reigned for six years, with defences on three continents, including two in Canada in 1931. Strangely, given the time taken to cross the Atlantic in those days, his solitary contest between the two Montreal bouts came before some 8,000 people in the Cynon Valley.

Welsh fans had their first sight of Brown when he and his opponent were introduced from the ring in a show at Ammanford, where Ginger Jones had settled after leaving his native Rhondda. The contrast between the lanky black champion, wearing a grey check suit with plus fours, and the pale, 5ft 4in local brought gales of laughter from all concerned.

And the physical disparity naturally played a major part in the outcome when they came together for business a few days later. Jones, one of three boxing sons of a Ferndale mountain fighter, was good enough to have occupied the Welsh featherweight throne for the previous two years, but his domestic supremacy did little to prepare him for Brown.

Despite the difference in class, Al had insisted that Jones made the agreed nine stone, forcing him to shed a surplus pound. Given that Brown himself was only half a pound inside the feather limit, it seemed an unnecessary precaution.

With a seven-inch height disadvantage, Ginger had little alternative but to target the body and hammer away at close quarters. It proved a reasonably successful strategy, too, with Al finding it difficult to keep his tiny tormentor at bay, although his speed and variety of punch meant that he always looked in command.

Surprisingly, it was not the long-range work that brought the breakthrough for the taller man. He repeatedly bent low to whip shots up into Ginger's midriff and by midway they were taking effect. In the seventh of this scheduled 15-rounder a right to the ribs dropped Jones for nine. On rising, he was greeted by a barrage which felled him twice more, each time for seven, before the bell came to his aid.

A one-sided eighth session saw the Welshman further weakened and the ninth saw the end. A volley to head and body had Ginger in trouble, before a right to the pit of the stomach sent him crashing in agony, unable to beat the count. There were complaints from his corner and further afield that the final blow had been south of the border – Ginger proclaimed as much until his dying day - but these were rejected by referee Bill Allen.

For Jones, it was back to the workaday fare. He kept his Welsh title for another two years, until weight-making became too difficult, and ill-health soon brought an end to his career. He turned his hand to training youngsters, while earning a crust in insurance. He died at Pontardawe at the ripe old age of 81.

Brown's bones are now back in his native Panama

His conqueror was not so fortunate. After losing his world honours to Spaniard Baltazar Sangchilli, Brown hung up his gloves, but reconsidered and launched a comeback which culminated in a revenge victory to reclaim his crown. But making bantam was now beyond him and he soon relinquished it, although there were sporadic appearances in the US and Panama for a few more years.

In retirement, Al struggled against cocaine addiction and died, penniless, from tuberculosis at the age of 48. Although buried in New York, his remains were later transferred to an impressive tomb in Panama City.

23

ALBERT	vs.	PETEY
BARNES		**SCALZO**

| **JULY 2, 1935** | **Yankee Stadium, New York** |

Between the wars amateur boxing was a big thing, both in Wales and in the States. But, even with club shows in Cardiff regularly attracting packed houses, Albert Barnes was stunned to find himself introduced to 48,000 people at New York's iconic Yankee Stadium.

For a 22-year-old from the working class community of Splott it was a real eye-opener. But Albert opened a few American eyes as well, handing out a masterclass to a local teenager who was good enough to become a world ruler in the professional ring a few years later.

Barnes was a two-time Welsh champion, adding the 1934 British ABA title in London. But the following year he lost a disputed decision in the semi-final to Laurie Case, a machinist from Darlington, and was only the second-string bantamweight when a Great Britain team set sail to face a team of New York Golden Gloves winners on their own patch.

As Albert and his colleagues trained in a specially erected American-style ring on the deck of the *Majestic*, Peter Donato Scalzo was a late addition to the line-up awaiting them.

Albert Barnes

Still a month shy of his 18th birthday, the lad from the Lower East Side had been boxing for less than two years, though the big right hand he had honed at the Yorkvilleites club had already brought him Metropolitan honours. A newsboy, he was regarded as something of a comedian, fond of practical jokes, and was a popular figure on the scene in the Big Apple.

The New York press had given Barnes a big build-up and he fully lived up to expectation. His opponent came out full of positive intent, as though he planned to hustle Albert out of his rhythm, but the Cardiffian, cool and unflustered, evaded his rushes with ease. In the second round, Barnes floored Petey, though the local rose immediately and landed a good right to the body.

Albert was totally on top, however, and frequently had Scalzo covering up on the ropes. The third saw Petey shipping regular punishment and he was exhausted at the final bell. Barnes's "chopping block right hook slowed the New Yorker down plenty", agreed a local reporter.

Although Barnes's fellow-Cardiffian, Jackie Pottinger, went down on

Petey Scalzo

points to Scottish-born George Coyle, an usher at the famous Radio City music hall, he played his part in what locals described as "the best flyweight bout, amateur or pro, seen in New York this year".

With Albert's bantam rival, Case, also winning, the Brits took the match by eight bouts to three. Not that they let their success go to their heads.

The great sports writer, Paul Gallico, was amazed at the phlegmatic way in which the visitors greeted their triumph, exemplified by ABA president Bill Dees when Gallico congratulated him afterwards.

"I said, 'Gee whiz, Bill, aren't you glad you won? Aren't you steamed up at all after travelling 3,000 miles and whipping us on our own home grounds?' He pulled on a cigarette for a moment and replied, 'I'm quite satisfied. Yes, I may say that I am satisfied.' What a people!"

There was certainly no lack of enthusiasm when the victorious party were welcomed back at Waterloo station. And its members were full of praise for the way they had been treated by their hosts.

Yankee Stadium

"I could have done with another week of it," said Albert, before returning to his humdrum world as a packer at Spiller's flour mill. There was one more important foreign adventure to come, however, with a trip to the Berlin Olympics, at which Barnes beat a Czech before losing a highly controversial decision to the eventual bronze medallist from Mexico.

Young Scalzo achieved revenge when the New Yorkers visited London in May 1936, outpointing an out-of-condition Barnes – although GB still won 7-4 – but the following month made his bow in the paid ranks with a first-round knockout.

Petey, growing into a featherweight, cut a swathe through the opposition until, on May Day 1940, he was recognised by the National Boxing Association as their world champion. He reigned for 14 months until knocked out by Californian Richie Lemos, later becoming a referee and serving as deputy boxing commissioner for New York State.

Despite plenty of offers, Barnes never turned pro, preferring the security of a steady job in the unpredictable 1930s. When war broke out, he became a paratroop instructor in the Royal Air Force, occasionally donning the gloves for action, but by the time peace arrived he considered himself too old for a serious ring return. He worked for Sherman's football pools and later had a betting shop in the Tremorfa area of his home city.

24

****

RONNIE JAMES vs. JACKIE WILSON

| JANUARY 12, 1936 | Blackfriars Ring, London |

****

Nat Fleischer, one of boxing's most revered journalists, was appalled. The founder of *Ring* magazine was in London with world-class American featherweight Jackie Wilson and he had just seen the youngster who was to cross gloves with his charge.

"This fight can't go on," insisted Fleischer. "It would be manslaughter." The object of his concern was an 18-year-old former boy soprano from Bonymaen, on the outskirts of Swansea, who had retained his choirboy looks. But if Nat, a renowned historian, had studied Ronnie James's record he might have been less keen to write him off.

Encouraged by his shopkeeper father, himself an amateur boxer, young Ronald learned the basics from a top tutor. Dai Curvis was to guide two of his sons, Cliff and Brian, to titles and the link-up with James had already borne fruit.

Despite his youth, Ronnie had had more than 50 contests and was yet to taste defeat. Fleischer should have known better.

But he was right to have faith in his own man. Born in South Carolina, but raised in Pittsburgh, Wilson – nine years James's senior – had been in Britain for a couple of months and had proved clearly superior to those locals he had so far encountered, including another Welshman, Merthyr's former Olympian, Cuthbert Taylor.

The visitor could be forgiven his confidence, even if the slogan embroidered on the white silk robe he wore into the ring was perhaps a little over the top. "Unofficial

Ronnie James

champion of the world", it claimed. Jackie continued his mind games with an ear-splitting war whoop, before crossing to the James corner and whispering, "Don't worry, son, it won't be long now."

Jackie Wilson

In the opening exchanges of their scheduled 10-rounder, it seemed Wilson's patronising attitude might be justified. His fleetness of foot gave Ronnie a few problems, while, despite his longer reach, Jackie's best work was done at close quarters. But by the midway point of the second, the Swansea lad had begun to find holes in the visitor's defence.

There was a little too much clinching involved and the third saw the referee abandon his ringside position to climb through the ropes and assume closer control of affairs. Both men responded by increasing the pace, James catching his rival with a solid right late in the round, from which Wilson did well to recover quickly.

Ronnie was making the American miss wildly at times, but Jackie landed enough for a mouse to appear on the home fighter's cheek, which swelled rapidly. His left eye was completely closed for the last five sessions, but the restricted vision seemed not to affect James's ability to measure his blows and his left lead was rarely out of Wilson's face.

The teenager's tireless workrate reached a peak in the final round, with two crunching hooks to the jaw halting the Pennsylvania fighter's increasingly desperate attacks. Jackie was so exhausted at the end that he slid to the canvas as his tormentor was pulled off him. There was never any doubt about the verdict.

Wilson won another seven contests while in the British Isles – including victories over two Welshmen, Cardiffian Doug Kestrell and Maesteg's Stan Jehu – before returning home and eventually justifying his dressing-gown boast by dethroning NBA feather king Richie Lemos in November 1941. He reigned for 15 months before losing the belt to Canadian ex-Olympian Jackie Callura, later moving to California and continuing his career until 1947.

Like so many boxers in that medically unregulated era, Wilson spent his last years in a mental institution, dying there in 1966 at the age of 55.

James's unbeaten record was to last a mere fortnight more, ending when a low blow brought his disqualification against Londoner Dave Crowley, who went on to win the British lightweight title.

But Ronnie's time would come, as we shall see.

25

★★★

TOMMY
FARR

vs.

TOMMY
LOUGHRAN

JANUARY 16, 1936	Albert Hall, London

★★★

An astute manager can be worth as much to a boxer as a knockout punch. Or so it would seem, if a top journalist is to be believed. For, according to legendary *Daily Mirror* correspondent Peter Wilson, the actions of Tommy Farr's handler, Ted Broadribb, turned defeat into victory.

Broadribb, a bricklayer's son from Walworth who, under the name Young Snowball, was good enough to stop a teenage Georges Carpentier, had not long been in the Farr camp. Young Tommy had laced on the gloves while just 13, desperate to add a few bob to the household budget after his widower father became bed-ridden following a stroke. At 16 he had earned enough to buy the family home in Blaenclydach.

Tommy Farr

Starting out as a flyweight, Farr moved through the weights, eventually becoming Welsh light-heavyweight champion and losing on points in a British title clash against Londoner Eddie Phillips. He then moved to Slough, lodging at the Dolphin Hotel, which had a gym on the premises, and Broadribb took over the business side.

A victory in Paris impressed American promoter Jeff Dickson and when the impresario brought Tommy Loughran to Europe he turned to Farr to occupy the stool in the opposite corner. The 'Phantom of Philly' was 33 and more than five years had passed since he relinquished the world light-heavy crown to mix it with the big boys, only to lose a highly suspect challenge to the Mafia-manipulated Primo Carnera.

But he was unbeaten in his last seven fights, including a points win at Wembley over New Zealander Maurice Strickland, when he came face to face with Farr over 10 rounds. The American raised a few eyebrows with some pre-fight comments, but if the crowd – which included more than 100 miners who had travelled from the Rhondda in the back of four lorries - entertained any feelings of antagonism at the first bell, they had been replaced by those of sympathy, mixed with incredulity, at the end.

Loughran was sporting something of a spare tyre, which immediately attracted Farr's belligerent attention. But for all the Rhondda man's success to the body, it was the transatlantic Tommy who caught the eye, responding with a variety of sharp and accurate counters and evading punches with the most subtle of movements.

A regular supply of uppercuts, from both left and right, jolted Farr's head back, although Loughran

Was Tommy Loughran robbed?

lacked the power to inflict significant damage. The home fighter's fitness showed in a strong finish, but he was still being made to miss as often as he landed.

Although Farr had performed better than many had expected, there were few who considered he had done anywhere near enough. This was where, it seems, Broadribb earned his percentage. He jumped into the ring and ran to Farr, loudly telling him, "You skated it!" According to Wilson, inexperienced referee Wilfred Smith, who had been moving towards Loughran, abruptly changed direction and raised the Welshman's arm. Others, it must be recorded, saw no such hesitation.

It took a second or two to sink in, but then the chorus of dissent tested the hall's renowned acoustics to the full. The poor MC took the brunt, the referee having briskly left the ring. The Americans protested, only to be told that the third man's decision was final.

Despite his disappointment, Loughran fought twice more in Britain, losing to Ben Foord and beating Jack London, before returning to North America, where he boxed on for little more than a year. In later life he became a successful player in the more sedentary pursuit of bridge, dying in 1982 at the age of 79.

26

★★

TOMMY		BOB
FARR	**VS.**	**OLIN**

APRIL 2, 1936	Albert Hall, London

★★

The victory over Tommy Loughran was there in black and white on Tommy Farr's record, no matter how many thought it fortunate. But even the Welshman's greatest admirers accepted he needed further education in the matter of handling American opposition.

Bob Olin

Bob Olin seemed like an ideal teacher. Like Loughran, the Brooklynite had ruled the world's light-heavyweights, losing the crown to John Henry Lewis just six months earlier, and he had travelled to London to test himself out against the big boys.

A former law student, Olin changed direction to work on the New York stock exchange as a broker. It paid off, too, as he made himself a small fortune in quick time. But then came the slump and Bob's bank balance took a big hit. A former Golden Gloves champion, he looked to the ring to reclaim some of his losses.

After just four years as a pro, Olin took the world title from 'Slapsie' Maxie Rosenbloom, but reigned for less than a year before being outpointed by Lewis. Bob blamed the strain of shedding nearly a stone in the few days before the bout and turned his gaze to the heavyweights.

London's fight crowd were told the visitor would be crossing gloves with Farr's nemesis, Londoner Eddie Phillips, but the announcement was premature, while the reported date was ruled out as Olin would not box on a Jewish holy day. In the end it was Tommy in the other corner on Jeff Dickson's card a few days later.

Bob brought a completely different skill-set to that of Loughran. Where the Philadelphian was a master of defence and technically proficient, Olin used his mobility to move in close and throw clubbing hooks, bearing power in both hands. In addition, he felt lucky: in the previous week he had backed the winner of the Lincoln and cleaned up in two sweepstakes on the Grand National. It did not last.

Farr set a tremendous pace from the first bell, although the American landed a left hook in the closing seconds of the opener which nicked Tommy above the right eye. The Welshman's straighter punching was proving invaluable, his left regularly in Bob's face, although a left swing dropped the home fighter for an instant in the fifth, his recovery so immediate that the timekeeper did not get a chance to count.

As the pair moved into the second half of the 10-rounder, Olin started to fire his hooks more frequently and an all-out attack in the ninth ended with a right over Tommy's too-low hands, which sent him to the canvas. This time he was clearly hurt, although he was up at two and survived until the interval.

A torrid last session saw Olin launch a desperate assault in a bid to put things beyond doubt, but Farr's chin withstood the pounding and referee C.B. Thomas, from Maesteg, gave his fellow-countryman the nod.

Cue lamentation in the American camp. On returning to the privacy of the dressing-room, Olin broke down in tears at the injustice of it all. Manager Paul Damski protested volubly. And they had support in the crowd, even though the outrage never matched that following the Loughran affair.

"I consider I was robbed," lamented Bob. Damski went further. "Olin played with him as a master with his pupil," he insisted.

But most ringside scribes thought the Rhondda man's higher workrate and more accurate punching deserved the nod, with *Boxing* – which had condemned the outcome of Farr-Loughran - accusing Olin of posing. "The verdict went against him simply because he failed to carry into full effect all the many clever and crafty things he shaped to do," wrote editor Sidney Ackland.

Unconvinced, Bob headed back to the States, where he persuaded his body to make light-heavy once more for a rematch with Lewis, only to be halted in eight rounds. He boxed on until 1939, appearing in Canada and Australia, but never again in Britain. Olin ran a successful restaurant in Manhattan until his death from a heart attack in 1956, at just 48 years old.

27

I t would be fair to say that Tommy Farr was not the preferred choice of promoter Sydney Hulls when it came to finding an opponent for the colourful American's bow in a British ring. After all, he had not been getting rave reviews in recent outings.

The Rhondda man had finally been given the British title shot he craved. Cardiffian Jack Petersen, who had studiously ignored his fellow-Welshman's calls, had lost the Lonsdale Belt to South African-born Ben Foord and, in addition, with Farr at ringside, had just been halted for a third time by the German thorn in his side, Walter Neusel, ruling out any rematch.

Farr was duly paired with Foord and, boxing more cautiously than usual, outjabbed the taller man to take the title after 15 unexciting rounds. Baer was among those less than enthralled by the spectacle. And it did nothing to solve Hulls's conundrum.

Max Baer, the playboy pugilist

When he had signed up the American, he had visions of a bonanza night against the popular Petersen. Maximilian Adelbert Baer, born in Nebraska, but raised in California, was among the most talked about fighters of the day. He had attained the world heavyweight throne in 1934, flooring the giant Italian, Primo Carnera, repeatedly on the way to a points decision. One day short of a year later, despite being 10-1 on, he was himself outscored by the unsung James J. Braddock.

But it was his personality, as much as his ring achievements, that made Baer such an attraction. With charisma oozing from every pore and lovely ladies draped over each arm, Max had what would now be called "crossover appeal". People with little interest in the fight game knew who he was. He

had even starred in a feature film, *The Prizefighter and the Lady*, opposite star actress Myrna Loy.

Baer may not have been aware of it, but Myrna's real surname was Williams and her grandparents were Welsh. Now he was expecting to get up close and personal with another Welshman in Petersen.

But Jack abruptly announced his retirement at just 25, after being warned that retina damage threatened his sight if he carried on boxing. Foord's defeat by Farr ruled him out. And the Board vetoed a suggestion that Neusel should step in, insisting that two foreigners could not meet in a British ring. Hulls had to turn to Tommy.

In the event, he need not have worried. Farr produced an outstanding performance and the Harringay crowd – some 13,800, a British record for an indoor boxing event - were on the edge of their seats from the first bell. Baer's pre-fight wisecracks had irritated Tommy, who was also rather scornful about the American's garish robe, and he went straight on the offensive, a nick appearing near Max's right eye before the first round was over.

Farr (facing) outpoints Baer in a major upset

The Welshman was much faster than the somewhat sluggish visitor, who was unable to land with any of his vaunted power, while shipping regular lefts as he tried to move in. The cut became worse, while its owner struggled to keep up with the pace Tommy had set.

Realising he was well behind, Baer found some untapped reserves in the last two sessions, pleading with his tormentor, "Come on, Tommy, let's have a fight." Now supremely confident, Farr accepted the challenge and stood toe to toe with the American until the final bell was followed by referee C.H. Douglas's decision in his favour, greeted by massive cheers and an enthusiastic rendition of *Hen Wlad fy Nhadau*.

There were no protests from Max, who kissed the winner on the cheek in acknowledgement of a job well done, adding, "All I want now is a glass of beer." Tommy celebrated his triumph, back at his Blackheath training quarters, with a card game and a fish supper.

Baer stayed in Britain to outpoint Foord and was to gain revenge over Tommy when they met at Madison Square Garden a year later. He boxed on until 1941, but was never given a title shot at Louis, who had knocked him out before becoming champion. Max then concentrated on his acting career, dying at the age of 50 in 1959.

A smiling Baer embraces his conqueror

 **28**

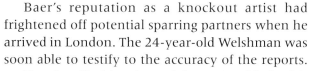

JIM **WILDE**	vs.	BUDDY **BAER**
MAY 6, 1937		Harringay Arena, London

Amonth after big brother Max faced Tommy Farr there, Buddy Baer - Jacob Henry to his parents - took on Welsh opposition of his own at the new 10,000-seat arena in North London.

Jim Wilde, from Swansea, was known as 'Big Jim' to avoid any unlikely confusion with the legendary flyweight and had underlined the size difference by winning the Welsh heavyweight title in 1935, though he lost it to the improving Farr the following year.

'Big' he may have been in comparison to his namesake, but he still conceded several inches to the 21-year-old visitor from California, whose 6ft 6in frame was sufficiently fleshed out for Wilde to be conceding nearly two and a half stone on the night.

Big Jim Wilde

Baer's reputation as a knockout artist had frightened off potential sparring partners when he arrived in London. The 24-year-old Welshman was soon able to testify to the accuracy of the reports.

Not that Buddy, cheered from ringside by his famous sibling, impressed too many outside the ropes as he moved ponderously forward in the early stages, eating Wilde's left hand with a supreme lack of concern. Midway through the opener, across came the American's right, down went Jim and the die was cast.

After a lengthy count, Wilde went on the retreat, but Baer landed another right and the whole scenario was replayed. A third knockdown followed, but this time the bell intervened to allow Jim to recover on his stool.

The second session saw a turnaround of fortunes, with one major difference. Wilde totally outboxed Baer, even landing a thumping right on his rival's jaw, but Buddy shrugged it off without blinking. Jim succeeded in evading the artillery firing in his direction, but without giving the impression that his defence was impregnable.

And the third saw Baer stagger Wilde several times before dropping him with a shot that also opened a cut over the Swansea fighter's left eye. Jim survived the round, but it was only a matter of time.

Buddy Baer

Realising the vulnerability of his foe, Buddy stepped up the pace and launched a two-fisted onslaught ending with a roundhouse left which deposited Wilde on his back, his legs in the air. He rose at two, but referee Moss Deyong called a halt without waiting for another blow to land. Jim protested volubly, but most observers found little reason to disagree with the decision.

The crowd appreciated the loser's gameness and cheered him to the echo, but his face was a mess as he made his way to the dressing-room.

Ironically, Buddy's only other bout in Britain was in Wilde's home town a couple of weeks later. He faced Englishman Jack London at the Vetch Field, winning a 10-round points decision, before heading back to the States and his eventual shot at glory against the immortal Joe Louis.

Their first meeting saw Louis knocked through the ropes in the opener, but he recovered to dominate, flooring a groggy Baer several times in the sixth. The last blow looked to land a split second after the bell and Buddy's manager, Ancil Hoffman, continued his arguments beyond the interval, his refusal to leave the ring prompting his man's disqualification.

The unsatisfactory ending guaranteed Baer a rematch, though there seemed little point. Eight months later Joe felled him three times and finished matters inside a round.

Buddy never boxed again, following his brother into bit-part appearances in films and television series, dying in 1986 at 71.

Wilde, meanwhile, extended his ring career until 1948, though with limited success in later years. He ran a drinking club near Swansea's main railway station, reaching the ripe age of 79 before hearing the final bell.

29

★★

TOMMY		JOE
FARR	**vs.**	**LOUIS**

AUGUST 30, 1937	**Yankee Stadium, New York**

★★

I t was the night Wales did not sleep. Or so runs the legend. Across the country, people huddled around crackling radio sets to hear the commentary of Canadian Bob Bowman as one of their own took on the fearsome 'Brown Bomber' for the heavyweight championship of the world.

Legendary rugby ace Cliff Morgan was taken by his parents to a field behind his home at Trebanog to join hundreds listening as the signal was amplified over loudspeakers. His grandfather, Isaac Christmas Morgan, was among fervent Welsh supporters cheering their hero from the Yankee Stadium bleachers. At home in Tonypandy, the Empire was jam-packed as Tommy's townsfolk gathered to follow events from more than 3,000 miles away.

Joseph Louis Barrow, the son of Alabama sharecroppers who had moved to Detroit when he was 10, had stormed through the ranks, leaving a series of fallen opponents behind him, to establish himself as a champion-in-waiting. But Louis was black – and in order to be given a shot he had to convince a doubtful America that he was not the second coming of Jack Johnson.

The big Texan, who claimed the title at the dawn of the century, had

offended a race-conscious society, flaunting both his wealth and his white mistresses, and for more than two decades the boxing establishment made sure there was no recurrence, refusing to countenance a black owner of "the biggest prize in sport". Louis's natural humility, allied to a carefully controlled public image – he was under strict orders never to be photographed with either white women or alcohol – began to win public support and, despite a shock knockout by German Max Schmeling, he duly demolished James J. Braddock to ascend the throne.

Fight impresario Mike Jacobs was now seeking his first

Farr lands a left lead on Louis

challenger. Farr's star was high after he followed up his victory over Max Baer with a stunning knockout of Jack Petersen's three-time conqueror, Walter Neusel, and he had been guaranteed £7,000 to meet Schmeling in London. But there were other irons in the German's fire: as the only man to beat Louis, the former champion reckoned he deserved a chance to repeat the feat – and regain the title into the bargain.

But the 'Black Uhlan' was asking for too much money. So Jacobs turned to Farr.

'Uncle Mike' spared no efforts in making his man welcome, either. He was allocated top-class training facilities at Long Branch, where the mayor, Alton Evans, perhaps influenced by his own Welsh blood, awarded him the freedom of the city. But Jacobs looked after his own interests as well, ensuring that Farr agreed to give Louis a rematch if, through some strange eventuality, he should dethrone him. It was the first of the notorious "return clauses" that became the norm in the postwar years.

Tommy was a gift to Jacobs's publicity machine, even if the champion was not sure what exactly he was about. Joe, noting the scars on Farr's back, mementos of his mining days, asked where they had come from. "I used to wrestle with tigers in a circus," replied a poker-faced Tommy.

Given that Farr was the first Briton in a generation to contest heavyweight supremacy, there was plenty of excitement back home. But the Board of Control did not join in, instead primly insisting that this was no more than an eliminator and that they would only recognise Tommy as champion if he then beat Schmeling. The National Sporting Club, however, left no doubt about their stance, donating an £800 gold belt for the winner.

There was a four-day delay because of bad weather before the pair came together. Farr had scaled 14st 8 1/2lb (204 1/2 in American terms), with Louis seven and half pounds lighter. There were 40,000 present to see Tommy, his silk dressing-gown bearing the dragon that Freddie Welsh had worn on his shorts when he became world lightweight king 23 years before, enter the ring, among them a group of Welsh fans in a special enclosure set aside "so that they could join in song" and marked by the national flag, provided by the *Western Mail*.

They had little to be vocal about in the opening rounds, as Farr took a long look at the task at hand. The third saw the Welshman begin to land at close range, but he found it difficult to get past Joe's immaculate left and finished the session cut beneath both eyes.

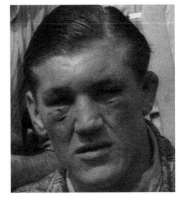

Tommy shows the scars of battle

The two rivals talk over old times

Those who had predicted a quick finish began to waver as Tommy's movement kept him clear of the champion's explosive right fist. When the American did get through, in the fifth, it seemed to have minimal effect, a collective gasp revealing the surprise of those watching. Not that Farr would agree.

"He was dynamite," he admitted, afterwards. "When he hit you it was like being in the middle of an explosion."

As the pair entered the second third of what even those scornful of Britain's "horizontal heavyweights" were beginning to accept was a bout likely to last the full 15 rounds, Tommy began to land some bombs of his own. The bell came to Joe's aid at the end of the sixth, when two lefts and a right had him in a certain amount of trouble. Mind you, the experience served to stir Louis into delivering a bit of a battering in the next session and, despite a stirring recovery from the challenger, he was bleeding heavily by the 10th.

There was still time for Farr to cut Louis near the right eye as he staged a 12th-round onslaught and after a couple of evenly matched rounds it was the Rhondda man on top in the final exchanges. There were few complaints when Louis had his arm raised, with the gallant loser agreeing - "I thought he just shaded it" – and blaming his own inactivity in the early stages.

Louis was to reign for a record 12 years, with Farr the first of 25 successful defences, until defeat against Jersey Joe Walcott saw him call it a day. Tommy, one of his regular disputes with the Board prompting him to discard his British title, continued to campaign in the US, although out-of-ring distractions contributed to four straight losses. Soon afterwards, ill-health brought his retirement.

But he and Louis were each to come back, financial woes forcing them to lace up the gloves again. Farr was reasonably successful, becoming Welsh champion before a former blacksmith from Battersea, Don Cockell, halted him in a British title eliminator. Joe battled on until he was demolished by an unbeaten youngster called Rocky Marciano.

Tommy's return had solved his money worries and he became a respected pundit, living in his adopted Sussex until his death from cancer on St David's Day, 1986, at the age of 72.

Louis, however, never escaped his debts – mostly owed to the unforgiving US tax department – and in later life suffered the consequences of carrying on too long, his mental decline aggravated by drug addiction. For years he earned bed and board by greeting gamblers at Caesars Palace in Las Vegas, eventually succumbing to a heart attack in 1981, aged 66.

30

★★★

RONNIE **JAMES**	VS.	IKE **WILLIAMS**
SEPTEMBER 4, 1946		**Ninian Park, Cardiff**

★★★

Despite the long tradition of boxing in Wales, never before had the country hosted a fully recognised world championship bout. Suddenly, amid the postwar explosion in sporting attendances, Ninian Park – where Cardiff City were just setting out on a season which saw them top the old Third Division (South) – was to witness a Welshman contesting global supremacy on home ground.

Ronnie James, the boy from Bonymaen, had come a long way since announcing himself to the Americans by beating Jackie Wilson back in 1936. He had become British lightweight champion, knocking out Eric Boon two years earlier at the Welsh capital's other sporting cathedral, Cardiff Arms Park.

There had also been a spell in khaki, including service in France, where the story nearly came to a premature end. James was stranded at Dunkirk, his bootless feet bleeding and swollen, until a familiar face appeared over the horizon. Glen Moody, the Welsh light-heavyweight champion, picked up his crippled countryman and carried him on his back, pack and all, until he could transfer him to an Army lorry.

Meanwhile, across the Atlantic, there was a new monarch in the lightweight division. The family of Georgia-born

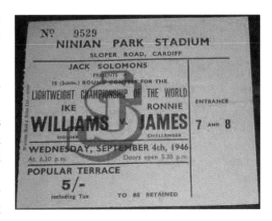

Five bob let you see Wales's first world title fight

73

The Lord Mayor of Cardiff, Walter Wills, welcomes Ike Williams and his wife

Isaiah 'Ike' Williams headed for New Jersey when he was young and he learned to fight as a Trenton newspaper seller, defending his pitch against rival entrepreneurs. He turned pro in 1940 and five years later claimed the NBA version of the world title by knocking out Juan Zurita in a Mexico City bullring.

Not that he ever wore the symbol of his success. Mexican fight fans are not renowned for their magnanimity in defeat and a bottle-throwing mob stormed the ring, one of their number taking the belt back at gunpoint. After that, Williams was hardly likely to worry unduly about a trip to Wales.

Ike, wife Virginia, manager Connie McCarthy and trainer Harry Curley flew in – itself something of a change from the traditional week on a ship – with the champion keener to talk about golf than the upcoming fight. He based himself in London to try out some local courses before heading west.

Not that it was great golfing weather. There had been steady rain in Cardiff and the forecast for the big day saw no improvement. Promoter Jack Solomons was unworried. "I'm going to get a pair of sun-glasses for each spectator," he vowed. "It's going to be a beautiful night." His optimism proved justified, but there was nothing beautiful about it for James.

Williams, perhaps preoccupied with his putting – and upset at being unable to find oranges in postwar Britain - had neglected his gym work and spent the eve of the fight buried in layers of clothing in a bid to beat the scales, but came in more than a pound over. After a last strenuous workout, he shed the final ounces, but his difficulties must have boosted Ronnie's self-belief. It was clutching at straws.

More than 40,000 filled the terraces, but such was the general apprehension that even the renowned St Alban's Band found little response to their attempts to get them singing. The champion seemed affected by the general lethargy in two uneventful opening rounds before a James uppercut in the third jolted him into activity. Unable to get past Ike's long arms, Ronnie altered his tactics and tried to work inside; the American tied him up with ease.

The sixth saw referee Moss Deyong warn both men for straying near the kidneys, but the challenger's sins were due to increasing desperation.

A left hook dropped the Welshman in the seventh and in the next Williams uncorked his famous 'bolo punch', starting at head-height and describing a circle before being whipped in from his hips and landing beneath the victim's heart.

On three occasions James crumpled in agony from such shots, but somehow carried on each time and before the end of the round landed a left to the head, which brought a rare cheer from the stunned fans. It was a token gesture.

Down and almost out - Ronnie's dream is done

Ronnie had vowed to counter the 'bolo' with something he called his 'Cwm Rhondda' punch, but the "strong deliverer" was in the opposite corner.

Another body assault felled James early in the ninth and a barrage to the head sent him down again. As he drew himself upright, a thunderous right to the jaw spun him around and dropped him over the bottom rope.

A befuddled Ronnie crawled forwards before managing to get to his feet only to find the count had been completed. He was, in any case, in no state to continue.

"Ike is a real champion," admitted the Welshman afterwards. "He was punching too hard and I had to concentrate too much on defence. If only this fight could have been staged eight years ago."

The victor provided the back-handed compliment that Ronnie had been "much harder to beat than I thought he would be". But he paid tribute to his rival's left hook. "I tasted that punch early on," he said, "and afterwards I made quite sure he didn't hit me with it again."

Williams returned home to halt rival claimant Bob Montgomery and establish himself as the undisputed ruler until he was dethroned by Jimmy Carter in 1951. But the sticky fingers of Mafia boss 'Blinky' Palermo, who had taken over control of his career, meant Ike saw little of the proceeds, a point he underlined when courageously testifying before the Kefauver Commission into organised crime.

James could no longer make lightweight and hung up his gloves after being stripped of his domestic honour. He dabbled with promotion and management before emigrating to Australia, where he became a referee and worked as a masseur to a top rugby league club.

31

★★★

EDDIE
THOMAS

VS.

BILLY
GRAHAM

| FEBRUARY 7, 1949 | Harringay Arena, London |

★★★

The coming months were to see the name of Billy Graham become known around the world. The young evangelist attracted the support of newspaper magnate William Randolph Hearst and his sermons were broadcast to huge audiences. But at the start of 1949, the only Billy Graham most Americans were aware of was the 26-year-old son of a saloon keeper from Manhattan's East Side.

A pro since his teenage years, Graham had built an impressive unbeaten run spanning his first 58 fights – although there were a handful of draws along the way – and while he had lost three times before visiting Britain, he was still regarded as a certain future champion.

Eddie Thomas's left lead immortalised in bronze

Eddie Thomas, raised in a terraced cottage above Merthyr, had similar dreams, with plenty of good judges reckoning he would become Wales's first world titleholder since the glory days of Welsh and Wilde. A former amateur star, he moved quickly through the pro ranks, but lost a British championship eliminator to exiled fellow-countryman Gwyn Williams.

He nevertheless beat veteran holder Ernie Roderick in a non-title encounter before revenge over Williams earned him the Welsh crown. Eddie was back in the mix for a shot at the Lonsdale Belt. But promoter Jack Solomons felt the youngster was destined for bigger prizes and brought the highly touted Graham to test out his theory.

The cigar-smoking deal-maker proved justified. But it was far from straightforward. Thomas's ramrod left jab was the basis for all his work and it found a regular home in the American's face throughout the 10 rounds. Yet Graham was also endowed with more than usual skill and there were periods when he outboxed the comparatively inexperienced Welshman.

Eddie bled from the nose from an early stage, testimony to Graham's successes, but the visitor's attempts to get inside Thomas's longer arms were generally fended off. By the fifth Billy was marking up above the left eye and the bruising soon developed into an egg-like swelling which impaired his vision on that side.

Graham's lack of a big punch also hindered him as he endeavoured to alter the course of the bout, with Eddie dominating the closing stages and taking a clear-cut decision.

Billy Graham

It was only when the celebrations died down that the truth emerged: while Graham's nervous system registered every one of Eddie's lefts, the puncher himself had felt nothing. After damaging the hand in training, Thomas had an injection before the fight to freeze the fist. It worked well enough on the night, but had consequences, both short- and long-term.

While the jubilant Merthyr man headed home on the midnight train – he snubbed a paid-for first-class sleeper to sit in third class with his fellow miners – Solomons and manager Sam Burns were fielding phone calls from across the Atlantic. Over the next few days, there were offers for a Stateside rematch with Graham and an invitation to face highly rated Charley Fusari at Madison Square Garden. The injured mitt meant none could be accepted.

Eddie never did get to fight in America. He never contested the world crown, either, despite attempts by Solomons to tempt the great Sugar Ray Robinson to defend in Britain. But, despite regular hand trouble, he won British, Empire and European titles to put himself in the pantheon of Welsh boxing immortals.

Graham had to wait two years for his own opportunity and the odds were stacked against him, even in his home city, when he challenged Kid Gavilán. Although most ringsiders saw Billy a clear winner, the 'Cuban Hawk' was awarded a split decision.

Thomas (right) moves in on Graham

Graham's manager, Irving Cohen, had apparently refused a pre-fight "request" to transfer a percentage of Billy's contract to underworld figure Frankie Carbo and it was alleged that Carbo's associates had leaned on at least one of the judges. But there were no such claims after Gavilán again outpointed the New Yorker in Havana in 1952.

Billy retired three years later, having never been floored in 126 pro bouts, and became a referee and judge, while earning a living as a representative for Seagram's whisky. He died of cancer in 1992, aged 69.

For Thomas, true greatness came after he hung up his gloves. He proved an outstanding teacher, guiding fellow-townsman Howard Winstone and Scot Ken Buchanan to world titles and earning worldwide fame as a cutman. Beyond the ropes, the man who worked underground his whole life was elected Mayor of his beloved Merthyr before cancer took him, too, in 1997.

Harringay Arena - and the other Billy Graham tops the bill

32

★★★

JOHNNY
WILLIAMS

VS.

GEORGE
KAPLAN

NOVEMBER 14, 1950	Earls Court, London

★★★

Like most boxers, New Yorker George Kaplan regarded it as a bonus if he was able to put his opponent to sleep. But for his manager, that outcome was essential to his work. He was a professional hypnotist.

Jimmy Grippo had other skills, too, and once entertained the denizens of Stillman's Gym by relieving the fearsome proprietor of his watch as they shook hands. While apologising, he then lifted the man's wallet. But as Lou Stillman pointed out, "What's so great? He once picked President Hoover's pocket in the White House!"

Grippo was no mug when it came to boxing, mind. He had guided Melio Bettina to the world light-heavy crown in 1939 and had similarly big ambitions for Kaplan – if he could impress against Johnny Williams.

The Williams family had moved to Rugby from their farm near Barmouth and young Johnny had to learn to fight from an early age. When you're a five-year-old starting school in the English Midlands and you speak only Welsh, acceptance by your peers is unlikely to be instant. But his facility with his fists soon discouraged any overt hostility from his new classmates.

It also provided an unexpected source of pocket money as he grew older. Johnny was only 10 when he began boxing in the fairground booths, sneaking away from disapproving parents. By 19 he was a legitimate part of the boxing boom that greeted the end of World War II.

He became chief sparmate to top light-heavy Freddie

Johnny Williams and manager Ted Broadribb

George Kaplan

Mills and signed up with the Bournemouth man's manager, Ted Broadribb, who sent him to South Africa to build himself up to a full heavyweight away from the restrictions of ration-book Britain. When he returned, he was soon in the championship mix.

But progress was halted when Williams was cut and stopped by American Pat Comiskey and there followed a bloodstained points loss against another farm boy, Jack Gardner, in a British title eliminator. Broadribb looked across the Atlantic for Johnny's rehabilitation.

He came up with Kaplan. A son of Brownsville, the Brooklyn neighbourhood later to spawn Mike Tyson, George hardly had the most auspicious start to ring life, losing his first two bouts. But he had won 19 in a row since then, twice overcoming a Bronx namesake of Johnny Williams, before heading for Britain.

And he, like the Welsh Johnny, had been put on a weight-gain regime by the wily Grippo, who sent him into the hills with trainer Dan Florio, out of the reach of his big-city buddies and their tempting lifestyle.

It made little difference in London. On the bill which saw rival Gardner dethrone veteran Bruce Woodcock to claim the Lonsdale Belt, Williams showed that he, too, merited respect. His eyebrows still scarred from the battle with Jack, the Welshman was soon shedding more blood after Kaplan's opening right hand split an old wound on his left cheek. But his fans' anguish was misplaced; Johnny's elegant left was soon beating a tattoo on the visitor's features.

George, while enthusiastic and brave, lacked the basic skill to avoid the punches as he stalked Williams, occasionally throwing hopeful shots to the body. After four repetitive rounds, there were calls for the referee to rescue the increasingly battered American, but the bout was allowed to continue.

By the sixth Kaplan's right eye was almost closed and when he emerged from the corner for the seventh it was clearly his last hurrah. Johnny was supplementing the ramrod left with repeated rights and eventually the third man took the hint and called it off.

Kaplan returned home, but the spark was gone. Within 18 months he had hung up the gloves. Defeats can wreck fighters' dreams, but managers can always adapt. Grippo's reaction to events in London was to offer $25,000 for Williams's contract. Broadribb rejected it. And he gave the same reply to another prospective purchaser, film star Stewart Granger.

His faith was rewarded when Johnny went on to become both British and Empire heavyweight champion.

33

★★

JOHNNY		'HURRICANE'
WILLIAMS	**VS.**	**JACKSON**

APRIL 13, 1955	**Uline Arena, Washington**

★★

It was not the first time for the Welsh-speaking Midlander to display his wares in the US. Back in 1952, just after gaining revenge over Jack Gardner with a decision that earned him the British and Empire heavyweight titles, Johnny Williams had popped over to New Jersey and halted Albany's Jimmy Rousse in eight rounds.

But Rousse was already on the slide; his career lasted barely a year more. Tommy 'Hurricane' Jackson was a different proposition. Already ranked No 1 challenger to long-serving champion Rocky Marciano, he was a man in his prime.

He was only 24, five years younger than Williams, and had made his pro debut just eight days before Johnny, already six years into his career, beat Rousse. Originally from Sparta, Georgia, but long domiciled in New York City, he had little formal education and was a lonely, shy and inarticulate child.

But he soon found popularity in the ring, thanks to the energetic, unorthodox style that earned him his nickname. Far from unbeatable, he dropped decisions to spoilers such as Bert Whitehurst and Jimmy Slade and was defeated via the

Williams parades the Lonsdale Belt

Tommy 'Hurricane' Jackson

three-knockdown rule by the hard-hitting Cuban, Niño Valdés, who went on to stop four of Britain's top heavyweights, including Welshmen Dick Richardson and Joe Erskine, but was always sidestepped by the champion of the day.

But two points wins in a month over former ruler Ezzard Charles underlined Tommy's claims to contention and few expected any problems from Williams, who had lost his domestic belts to the fast-rising Don Cockell.

Johnny arrived in Washington a week before the fight and mixed runs along the banks of the Potomac with short sparring sessions. His sparmates were duly complimentary, former DC Golden Gloves winner Roland Randall insisting, "He boxes better and hits harder than Jackson. If his condition holds up, he'll win."

It didn't and he didn't. Although Williams denied that fitness was a factor, he did complain of tiredness. That had not been obvious in the opener, when the more skilful Welshman outboxed his man, but once Tommy stepped up the pace in the second the writing was on the wall. Johnny's footwork helped him avoid much thrown by the wild American, but things went dramatically wrong in the third.

Jackson, flailing indiscriminately, missed frequently, but the sheer volume of his punches eventually took its toll. Williams, forced to the ropes, tried to mix it, but with 15 seconds left in the session he collapsed under a renewed assault. Up at nine, blood streaming from a gash across the bridge of his nose, he was sent back to the canvas only for the bell to come to his rescue.

It was a matter of time in the fourth. Johnny lacked the strength to repel the rampaging 'Hurricane' and two solid rights and a subsidiary left dropped the fighting farmer on his face. Somehow he dragged himself to his feet, but referee Marty Gallagher noted the unsteady legs and waved it off.

"I'm afraid I've let everybody down," said Williams as he left the ring. "I'm just another Limey with a glass chin." He was assured by his listeners that he was not, but although his courage had garnered him new fans the emphatic nature of the loss dashed any slender hope of making his mark on the world scene.

Jackson lands a left

He returned home to a final shot at his old British title and a points loss to fellow-countryman Erskine in the rain at Cardiff's Maindy Stadium, followed by a six-round hammering from muscular Jamaican Joe Bygraves, convinced him enough was enough.

He moved into training, guiding George Aldridge to the British middleweight crown, but when his pupil retired Johnny also left the sport to focus on his farm. In later years he was a victim of Alzheimer's and died in 2007, aged 80.

Jackson never did face Marciano: just two weeks after Tommy's victory over Williams, the champion announced his retirement. Instead, 'Hurricane' was matched with a childhood acquaintance, Floyd Patterson, in a final eliminator and lost a split decision. After Floyd had beaten ancient Archie Moore for the vacant title, he offered his old friend a second chance, but won every round before ending matters in the 10th.

Tommy boxed on for another three years before calling it quits. He scraped a living shining shoes and driving a taxi until he was knocked down while cleaning his cab, suffering serious injuries. He never recovered, dying in hospital some six months later. He was only 50.

34

★★

DICK	vs.	EZZARD
RICHARDSON		**CHARLES**

OCTOBER 2, 1956	**Harringay Arena, London**

★★

The appearance on these shores of a former world champion was a rare event back in the days before the alphabet boys diluted the significance of the honour. So when the famed 'Cincinnati Cobra' came to town, he created quite a buzz. But the man did not live up to his billing. And his collision with one of Britain's most exciting fighters turned into, in the words of the *South Wales Echo* headline writer, "329 seconds of finger-wagging farce".

Georgia-born Charles began boxing as a middleweight in Ohio in 1940, moving through the weights to join the big men just as the legendary Joe Louis left the scene. Mind you, he still scaled under 13st when he outpointed Jersey Joe Walcott to ascend to the throne.

Dick Richardson

He beat Walcott in a rematch and outpointed Louis, when tax debts forced the great man back into the ring, before Jersey Joe dethroned him in their third meeting in 1951. Three years later he lost twice in challenges to the new star, Rocky Marciano – though he was the only man to last 15 rounds with him - and by the time he reached London he was clearly on the slide.

But, with more than 100 bouts on his record, he was still expected to see off a comparative novice. Richardson, known as the 'Maesglas Marciano' from the area of Newport in which he was raised, had opened his pro career with a points defeat against Henry Cooper's twin, Jim, and had more recently lost to fellow-Welshman Joe Erskine. He had seen off a selection of European imports, but this was his first tilt at someone from across the Atlantic.

Perhaps the pundits should have paid more attention

to the words of Charles's manager, Tom Tannas, who, while denying that his charge was "washed up", conceded that Ezzard might no longer have the ambition of old. "He is here strictly for the money," said Tannas, "having recently undertaken the purchase of a tavern, a sandwich stand and sundry other pieces of real estate in Cincinnati."

A capacity 14,000 crowd ignored the hint and packed the atmospheric arena, the biggest attendance at a show in the city for two years. They were sadly let down.

The first round brought no fewer than three stern warnings to Charles for wrestling, with Scots referee Frank Wilson taking him to his corner on one occasion to enlist the support of trainer Jimmy Brown. It had little effect. The second session simply brought more grappling and stumbling until the third man's patience ran out and he ordered the former champion back to his stool.

Ezzard Charles, former world champion

Ezzard seemed to find the whole episode amusing, grinning at newsmen as he left the hall. But he had his excuses ready when they spoke later.

"Richardson was using his head all the time," he insisted. "I was trying to push him off."

Dick, who was not totally innocent in the holding department, admitted, "I had to grab him sometimes to protect myself. But once I got him with a left hook to his ribs, he didn't want to know."

Tannas berated the referee for not giving the pair of them time to settle down and sort things out for themselves, while promoter Jack Solomons was so angry with Mr Wilson that he threatened to quit boxing unless the Board allowed him some say in the appointment of officials.

At least Richardson had a world champion's name in the 'W' column and could build on that. For the 35-year-old Charles, there were only half a dozen fights left before retirement.

His reputation, rightly, was unsullied by this aberration and earned him a place in the Hall of Fame. But a series of misguided investments forced him, ironically, to try wrestling for real. Sclerosis of the spine left him paralysed in later years and he died, virtually penniless, in 1975.

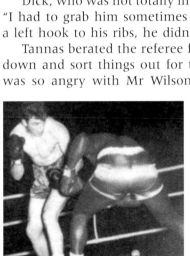

Some of what little action there was

35

★★

DICK
RICHARDSON
VS.
CLEVELAND
WILLIAMS

| **JULY 2, 1958** | **Coney Beach Arena, Porthcawl** |

★★

Scour the record books as much as you like: you will not find any mention of this fight. It never happened. But the story behind the non-event is one of the strangest in the history of a sometimes bizarre sport.

Sure, the pair had met at London's Empress Hall four months earlier, when Richardson, whose acknowledgement of the Queensberry Rules could be grudging at best, used his head more than his fists and was turfed out in the fourth by Frank Wilson, the same referee who had acted in the Newport man's favour when he disqualified Ezzard Charles.

It was decided they should try again and the rematch was made for Coney Beach – not the New York version, but its more modest namesake at Porthcawl, on the South Wales coast. Tickets went well: Dick was always popular and there was great interest in seeing the Texan farm boy with the knockout punch.

Williams had won 42 fights, with only two defeats – one of those avenged – and just six of his victories had required the judges to do their sums. Twelve opponents had not survived the first round. But the fans were not to see even that much.

The first inkling of a problem came with the weigh-in, set for 1 p.m. on the day of the fight. Richardson arrived at the gym above the fairground's Chamber of Horrors, but not the American, who was apparently unwilling to attend as the building had no central heating

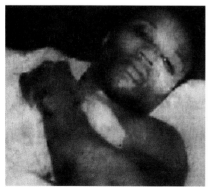

Cleveland Williams refuses to leave his bed

The programme cover was amended to show the new man ... but the inside still had Williams

– not something anyone else found a problem on a July day.

Williams insisted the ceremony should take place at his lodgings, the plush Brentwood Hotel, owned by Walker Cup golfer Graham Knipe. Dick shrugged his broad shoulders, strolled over to the hotel and tipped 14st 7lb (203lb) on scales placed on the thick carpet of the establishment's lounge. Still there was no sign of his rival.

One floor up, Cleveland lay in bed, claiming illness, while a dozen or more people argued across him. No fewer than four doctors, including the Board's own medical officer, rugby legend Jack Matthews, found nothing wrong and promoter Sir Leslie Joseph descended the stairs to announce to waiting journalists that the fight was on. Before the scribes could get to the phones, that was reversed.

With Williams's manager, Lou Viscusi, still in the US, trainer Bill Gore acted as spokesman for the fighter. First he blamed the weather. "When we left Texas the temperature was 101 degrees and we were told it would be much the same in Wales," he said. "We did not find it so."

Then, after claiming that Cleveland had "the sniffles" and could not train in a "dilapidated and dusty" gym, Gore changed tack and stunned his listeners.

"My boy has had a message from the beyond," he insisted. "Call it hoodoo or voodoo, he thought it would be bad for him to fight tonight."

Sir Leslie knew when he was beaten. He announced that the whole show would be postponed for a week, while South Wales Police despatched 50 extra officers to the arena in case of trouble from disgruntled fans. That never materialised, even though some coachloads had travelled from as far as London and Aberystwyth.

The following day the promoter had a long chat with the supposedly stricken boxer, emerging to proclaim that Williams looked like a new man and had vowed he would be ready for battle on the rearranged date. A day later and Cleveland actually rose and went for a run. It was a brief excursion; he quickly returned to the hotel and repaired once more to his sick bed.

A further medical examination found nothing amiss. Sir Leslie arranged for a specialist to take a look, but the Americans refused. In the morning, they left town and headed for Heathrow to fly home.

By this time, the irate promoter had been on the phone to Pittsburgh, where another of Richardson's former conquerors, Bob Baker, had been placed on stand-by. He jumped on a plane, presumably passing Williams somewhere over the Atlantic, and arrived in Wales, where he pronounced the weather "beautiful".

Mind you, it was raining by the new fight night and Baker, looking podgy despite having boxed 10 rounds three weeks earlier, never threatened to repeat his previous success, Richardson boxing intelligently to take a clear decision.

The British Board of Control banned Williams for life, calling for some similar sanction in the US, and ordered manager Viscusi to refund the money lost by Sir Leslie.

The Americans ignored them and Cleveland boxed on for another decade, despite losing a kidney after being shot by a traffic cop. He challenged for the world heavyweight title in 1966, but found Muhammad Ali at the peak of his powers and was stopped in three rounds. Williams died after being knocked down by a hit-and-run driver in 1999.

Richardson found unexpected success in Germany, where he halted local Hans Kalbfell to win the vacant European title, defending it on two return visits to Dortmund. He was dethroned by future world champion Ingemar Johansson and then knocked out by Henry Cooper in a showdown for domestic honours, prompting his retirement in 1963.

He ran a butcher's shop in Surrey for many years, dying in 1999, just two months before the man who refused to fight him.

36

★★

JOE	VS.	WILLIE
ERSKINE		**PASTRANO**

FEBRUARY 24, 1959	Wembley Pool, London

★★

The world title may have belonged officially to Floyd Patterson, but this was widely regarded as the match that would decide the best boxer in the heavyweight division. Perhaps neither had the power to see them to the ultimate prize – Erskine's fellow Cardiffians would admit that their man "couldn't punch a hole in a wet *Echo*" - but the pair were recognised, in Britain at least, as outstanding practitioners of the Noble Art.

A product of the dockland streets known worldwide as Tiger Bay, Joe Erskine was a naturally athletic youngster whose rugby skills earned him a Welsh boys' clubs cap as a fly-half. The same agility served him well in the ring, where he won a string of amateur honours before turning pro in 1956.

The son of a Jamaican-born booth fighter, Joe was still unbeaten when he won both British and Empire heavyweight crowns, but a retirement defeat to big-punching Swede Ingemar Johansson in a European challenge had been followed by the loss of his belts to a former amateur victim, Brian London. In both bouts Erskine had been hampered by cuts.

Top surgeon Emlyn Lewis was called in to resolve the problem with a skin graft above the left eye. His work passed its first test when Joe outclassed Frenchman Max Brianto. He was ready for Pastrano.

Wilfred Raleigh Pastrano was a podgy kid when he followed best friend Ralph Dupas to the neighbourhood gym in New

Joe Erskine, in life and in oils

Willie Pastrano

Orleans. Both would become world champions under the guidance of Miami-based Angelo Dundee, later to achieve legendary status as the mentor of Muhammad Ali.

'Will o' the Wisp' Willie shared with Erskine the conviction that it was far better to avoid being hit wherever possible. It led to the development of a style which was not designed to appeal to the blood-and-thunder tastes of the average American fight fan. But in Britain he found an appreciative audience.

There were points successes over a trio of home favourites - Welshman Dick Richardson, Jamaican-born Joe Bygraves and the pugnacious London - yet the local cognoscenti loved it. Willie even found many willing to support his complaint of a premature stoppage for a cut eye in a rematch with London.

The chance to see the brilliant visitor cross swords with the nearest British equivalent saw 12,000 pack out the Empire Pool. Promoter Jack Solomons was so enthused by the prospect that he arranged for the bout to be filmed in its entirety, so that it could be used in the instruction of would-be boxers throughout the country.

Such was the respect for Pastrano that Erskine began as a 3-1 underdog. And the Welshman had the worst possible start: even before the bell he was bleeding from a scratch on the nose caused by the thumbnail of a careless cornerman. Eight pounds heavier – though both were inside the present-day cruiser limit – Joe stayed out of range of Willie's jabs, while nipping in to land his counters.

And the tactics proved perfect. The Cardiff man varied the target for his left leads and his defence was watertight in the face of Pastrano's replies. By the fourth, Dundee's advice from outside the ropes was becoming increasingly urgent as his charge was seemingly unable to solve the Welsh conundrum.

Erskine was quick off his stool in each session, waiting for Willie to join him, and inevitably the first to strike. Even when the American landed his renowned double jab, Joe was able to respond with a fast combination to negate any advantage.

The last of the 10 rounds saw Pastrano hurling punches in desperation, but Erskine stood his ground, slipping the blows and giving back as many as he received. At the bell, Belfast referee Andy Smyth took a token glance at his scorecard before heading for the Welsh corner. There was no complaint from the American camp.

Indeed, Willie was generous with his praise. "Erskine is the best boxer I've

Pastrano blocks Joe's right

ever fought," he stressed, "and a mighty difficult man for anyone to handle."

The winner was, naturally, delighted. "After the first round I knew I had him beat," said Joe. "He hurt me several times, but he was always fighting the way I wanted him to."

Plans for Erskine to face Patterson went by the board when the New Yorker was dethroned by Johansson, launching a trilogy that tied up the world title for the next two years. Instead Joe focussed on domestic issues, but three times he fell short in British and Empire challenges to old rival Henry Cooper.

With the old cut-eye bugbear coming back to haunt him, Erskine battled on until defeat by the popular, but comparatively crude Billy Walker convinced him it was time to hang up the gloves.

By then Pastrano, having dropped a weight, was world light-heavy king, his defences including a stoppage of colourful Cockney Terry Downes. But the loss of his WBC and WBA crowns to Jose Torres prompted Willie, too, to call it a day.

He began a new life as a bit-part film actor, but picked up a drug habit and was in poor health until his death in 1997, at the age of 62.

Erskine had passed on seven years earlier. His retirement was plagued by illness, personal and financial problems and he died alone in a Cardiff flat, aged 57. An emotional docklands funeral demonstrated the city's affection for a man whose brilliance left opponents "trying to catch a moonbeam with tweezers", as one observer put it. If only he had had a punch to go with it.

37

DEREK RICHARDS vs. ROY McMILLAN

NOVEMBER 2, 1961	Wembley Pool, London

British fight fans of a certain age will never forget it. Their American counterparts, if they were ever aware of it, have no doubt consigned the night's events to a dark, rarely visited vault in their memory bank.

Back in the days when amateur boxing was a staple ingredient of Thursday night viewing on the BBC, a GB team took on the might of the US in what the visitors would call a "dual meet". Expectations were not great. In fact, the television people were mainly interested in making sure big-hitting heavyweight Billy Walker appeared during their allotted broadcasting time, so he was switched with the light-middle in a break from the traditional lightest-to-heaviest running order.

Derek Richards

'Blond Bomber' Walker did the business, flattening giant American Cornelius Perry inside a round. It took GB into a 7-0 lead and prompted high-level discussions at Broadcasting House. When an eighth home victory went into the books, the go-ahead was given: the cameras would keep rolling to let viewers across the land see if an unprecedented whitewash could be achieved.

The ninth Brit duly conquered and it was all down to that light-middleweight, switched to the final bout because the TV suits considered him expendable in their desire to showcase Walker. Suddenly Derek Richards was the man on whom history depended.

Originally from Merthyr, where he was born in a long-gone street below Brecon Road, Richards was

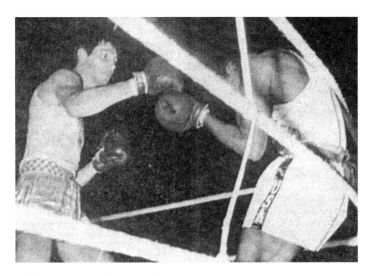

Richards has McMillan on the ropes

just four when his family moved to his mother's home town, Coventry, and it was in the Midlands that he learned to box. But the product of the Rootes club nevertheless wore the red of his native land in the international ring.

On this occasion, however, he had the whole of Britain behind him as he tackled a Golden Gloves champion from Toledo, Ohio, named Roy McMillan. And at first it looked as though the responsibility was proving too onerous, with the flashy visitor whipping in blows to the somewhat static Welshman.

But the second round saw Richards begin to target the body. His power had an immmediate effect, three consecutive right hooks downstairs almost folding McMillan in two and prompting the referee to step in and call a halt. Derek relaxed, his team-mates celebrated and the fans at Wembley and in living-rooms across the country went wild. Poor McMillan, on the other hand, was taken to hospital for treatment on suspected broken ribs.

Richards went on to win a Welsh ABA title in 1962 before signing with manager Wally Lesley and matching that triumph as a professional. He fell short, however, when it came to the British honour, losing in seven rounds to transplanted Dubliner Young McCormack.

McMillan, too, tried the paid game, but had limited success in a six-year career which saw him campaign in Canada and Italy as well as his homeland. He lost more than he won, although his rivals included the likes of Willie 'The Worm' Monroe, Tony Licata and future WBA ruler Miguel Angel Castellini.

38

BRIAN	vs.	EMILE
CURVIS		**GRIFFITH**

SEPTEMBER 22, 1964	Wembley Pool, London

Brian Curvis knew exactly what he was up against. Writing in the *Sunday Mirror* before his challenge for the world welterweight title, he proclaimed, "I have a date next week with a killer."

This was more than mere hyperbole. Two and a half years earlier, the Swansea man sat alongside promoter Jack Solomons at Madison Square Garden when Emile Griffith faced Benny 'Kid' Paret in a bid to reclaim the crown the Cuban had taken from him on a controversial decision six months before.

Brian Curvis

A Virgin Islander who moved to New York at 19, Griffith had an unlikely day job for a fighter: he worked in manager Howie Albert's business in the Manhattan garment district, designing women's hats. Such a sideline prompted suspicion from many in the sport and Paret was quite ready to give it voice.

At the weigh-in, Benny's gestures and repeated use of the Spanish word "maricón" underlined his opinion of Emile's sexuality. Griffith bottled his anger until they met in the ring, where he unleashed it in a frenzied assault which battered his man into semi-consciousness in the 12th round. Paret slipped into a coma and died in hospital 10 days later. And the whole tragedy was played out on live television.

Emile never really recovered from that night and suffered from nightmares for the rest of his life. But he had been able to block out the memories when it came to business and although he briefly lost his title to another Cuban, Luis Rodríguez, the Curvis contest would be the second defence of his third reign as champion.

Brian Nancurvis – the full surname, never used, testified to Cornish roots - was the fourth son of renowned trainer Dai. The two oldest saw their fistic dreams wrecked by the war, but the third, Cliff, won British and Empire belts. And the baby, 10 years younger, matched both those achievements.

In 31 pro fights, Brian had lost only once, a cut-eye defeat against American Guy Sumlin, later avenged. He could also point to a win over one of Griffith's unsuccessful challengers, Ralph Dupas; although it came via disqualification, Curvis had floored the New Orleans man, later to win world honours at light-middleweight.

Griffith's trainer, Gil Clancy, had visited Porthcawl to see Brian halt Johnny Cooke two months previously and agreed that the Welshman deserved a shot at his charge. He would be the first southpaw Emile had faced and his camp were worried enough to insist that the pair would have to use American gloves – and it cost Solomons £25,000 to clinch the deal.

Barbara, Curvis's bride of six months, was too frightened to attend, even after Griffith, worried about his "killer" label, had presented her with a personally crafted hat. There was no such reluctance from one celebrity fan: Frank Sinatra and his family were on hand to support the champion.

The rest of a packed house kept its collective fingers crossed that the Welshman's natural talent would be sufficient to cancel out the champion's experience. But the reality was obvious from the opening bell.

Curvis had been urged to take the initiative, but found himself forced back by a two-fisted onslaught as Emile made it clear who was the boss. And, despite sporadic success for the Swansea stylist, the pattern barely altered.

He repeatedly found himself with his back to the ropes. When he landed, the blows seemed to have no effect on the titleholder. Only in the sixth, when Curvis finally found his jab-and-move rhythm, did he enjoy a spell of superiority, but he was unable to maintain it as the relentless Griffith chased him down. By the end of the session, Brian had paid his first visit to the canvas.

Emile Griffith

Brian's face shows the pain of impending defeat

A body barrage – referee Harry Gibbs thought at least one effort was low and lectured the champion – had Brian hanging on in the eighth, although he recovered to land three successive blows to Emile's head two rounds later. But each time the West Indian was stung, he responded, and a one-two to the midriff sent Curvis down again.

A non-title encounter might have ended there, but Gibbs stayed his hand and Brian somehow found the reserves to dominate the 12th. It was a brief respite: Griffith dropped him once more in the next and although the challenger courageously saw matters through to the end, the referee's decision was never in doubt.

The Welshman acknowledged as much. "I lost to a far better man," he conceded afterwards.

Emile was more impressed by what went on outside the ropes. "How come, every time I knocked him down, they started singing?" he asked.

Curvis boxed on for two years, beating top men like Gaspar Ortega and Isaac Logart, but defeat in a bid for the European title, along with an acrimonious split from brother Cliff, prompted him to hang up the gloves. He later promoted in partnership with Swansea businessman Eddie Richards, before moving to Middlesbrough, where he died in 2012 after a long battle with leukaemia.

Griffith saw off two more challenges before moving up to middle and enjoying two reigns in that division, eventually retiring in 1970 to become a trainer. In later life, he acknowledged the truth behind Benny Paret's ugly insults, admitting that he was bisexual. In 1992 he was beaten up outside a gay club in New York, putting him in hospital for four months.

Emile, like Curvis, suffered ill-health in later years, finally taking his leave of us in the summer of 2013.

39

By rights, Howard Winstone should not even have been a professional fighter. As a 17-year-old factory worker, his right hand became trapped in a power press, ripping off the tops of three fingers. It seemed the boxing-mad teenager's ring days were over.

But, inspired by the way his father had overcome war wounds, the curly headed Merthyr boy vowed to stick with the sport and, making a virtue of necessity, focussed on developing what was to become one of the greatest left leads the game has seen. Maybe there were fewer knockouts on his record than there might have been without the accident, but the brilliant skill which compensated for his loss of power was key to him reaching the top.

Howard Winstone with promoter Bill Long

After winning host country Wales's only gold medal at the 1958 Empire Games, Winstone turned pro with his idol, Eddie Thomas, and stormed to the British and European featherweight titles. But there had been setbacks – and both involved Americans.

An unsung slugger from Saginaw, Leroy 'Honeyboy' Jeffery, knocked him out in two in front of the legendary Sugar Ray Robinson, who told Howard, "I had 40 fights before I was beaten, but I learned more from that defeat than from all the wins."

Fifteen months later Winstone had another educational experience when London referee Jack Hart controversially scored a 10-rounder in favour of a young body-puncher from Los Angeles, 'Gentleman' Don Johnson.

The Californian was always willing to travel, his early years including periods in Mexico and Australia, where former world bantam king Jimmy Carruthers was among

'Gentleman' Don Johnson

his victims. The success against Winstone marked his first trip to Europe.

Howard was now featuring in the world rankings, but the loss to Johnson was brought up each time anyone suggested him for a title shot. Eddie Thomas knew that the blemish on his reputation had to be erased. Merthyr publican Bill Long came up with the cash to tempt Don to Wales.

Johnson had just seen his own ambitions dented with a three-round loss in an Ecuadorian bull ring, but was confident that what he had done once he could do again. Winstone, still angry at the verdict first time around, was firmly of the opposite opinion.

Some 4,000 fans, crammed into the draughty old Market Hall, shared that optimism. They were encouraged when Howard stormed into the attack from the start, standing toe-to-toe in a way that clearly worried mentor Thomas. The unaccustomed aggression saw his pupil taking more than usual, with a cut opening along his left eyebrow in the third.

But, with that immaculate left constantly in Johnson's face in the fourth, any qualms in corner or crowd were dismissed as Winstone settled into a superb display of the finer arts. The Californian caught the eye with flurries in the seventh and eighth, but Howard toyed with his man in the closing sessions to leave no doubt in the mind of referee Ike Powell. Revenge had been achieved - and in some style.

The hall greeted the result with a passionate rendition of the national anthem and Johnson's manager, Joe Vella, was generous in his praise. "My guy lost to a great fighter," he said. "He should go to the States, he'd be a superstar."

Winstone never did appear in an American ring. But before the end of the year he had the first of his unforgettable trilogy against Mexican world champion Vicente Saldívar. Two close points defeats – many thought Howard had won their second meeting, in Cardiff – were followed by a painful stoppage loss at altitude in Mexico City.

But that fight was followed by Saldívar's surprise retirement – and Winstone halted Japanese Mitsunori Seki to claim the vacant throne. He was already on the slide, however, and lost the crown in his first defence, a stoppage at the hands of Madrid-based Cuban José Legrá bringing down the curtain on a glorious career.

Johnson had returned to Britain for a rubber match in Manchester, where he was harshly disqualified for persistent low blows. Defeats were now becoming frequent as Don yielded to a wanderlust unusual in American fighters, notoriously home-loving creatures.

His passport was stamped in 11 different countries – including Spain, where he was outpointed by Legrá - between the Carmarthen bout and his final outing, in South Africa in 1972. Incredibly, he never boxed in the US in that seven-year period, despite lacing up the gloves 40 times.

40

★★★

CARL		RAY
GIZZI	VS.	**PATTERSON**

JULY 12, 1966	Afan Lido, Aberavon

★★★

I t's true that Ray was never in the same league as big brother Floyd. But while his world heavyweight champion sibling was guaranteed a name check each time the younger man fought, in Britain at least he was recognised as a useful operator in his own right.

Having settled in Sweden – somewhat ironic, given Floyd's rivalry with local hero Ingemar Johansson – Ray had already paid two visits to these shores. At the National Sporting Club, he had outpointed the previously unbeaten Gizzi, returning to London to halt crowd-pleasing Midlander Johnny Prescott. Now he was to venture to Wales to face Gizzi again.

A descendant of Michael Angelo Gizzi, an itinerant ice cream vendor who left Italy in the 1880s and ended up in Rhyl a decade later, Carl had been inspired by watching Howard Winstone strike gold at the 1958 Empire Games in Cardiff. But he had already shown his mettle in a fight, overcoming polio, a crippling bone disease, double pneumonia and a ruptured hernia in a childhood which saw him in and out of hospital.

A Welsh champion at schools and senior level, he turned pro in 1964 with fellow North Walian Johnny Williams, but left the former British heavyweight king a year later to join his idol Winstone in the Merthyr gym of top trainer Eddie Thomas, who guided the rest of the 21-fight winning streak which had been snapped by Patterson three months earlier.

Ray himself was an outstanding amateur, claiming the Inter-City Golden Gloves trophy held the previous year by a certain Cassius Clay. His decision to base himself in Europe meant he was out of sight, out of mind as far as world title contention was concerned, but he still harboured ambitions of emulating Floyd.

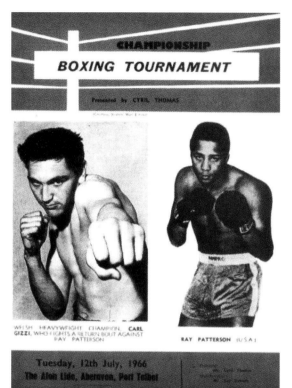

CHAMPIONSHIP
BOXING TOURNAMENT

Presented by CYRIL THOMAS

WELSH HEAVYWEIGHT CHAMPION, CARL
GIZZI, WHO FIGHTS A RETURN BOUT AGAINST
RAY PATTERSON

RAY PATTERSON (U.S.A.)

Tuesday, 12th July, 1966
The Afan Lido, Aberavon, Port Talbot
Official Programme - One Shilling

Gizzi, meanwhile, was driven by a thirst for revenge – their first encounter had been a short-notice affair - and a possible shot at British champion Henry Cooper. The mix attracted 3,000 to the seaside venue, with hundreds locked out, bringing a broad smile to the face of rookie promoter Cyril Thomas, brother of Eddie.

Carl had prepared well at Thomas's Penydarren sweatshop and looked much sharper than in their first meeting. Patterson, fleet of foot and fist, with the family's familiar peekaboo defence, resumed the hooking, aggressive style which had brought him success first time around.

But Gizzi kept his jab in the American's face and easily evaded whatever came the other way. By the fifth Ray's bruised face was reflecting the constant bombardment and optimistic ringsiders began talking of a possible knockout, especially when the visitor was cut in the eighth. The Welsh-Italian was, however, no big puncher and despite his efforts in the closing stages he was never able to floor his man.

At the bell to end 10 exciting rounds, there was no doubt whose hand would be raised. Carl had on occasion been criticised for a perceived negativity, but not this time. Alas, his passivity resurfaced in his next contests and he dropped decisions to Brazilian Renato Moraes and Argentinian José Menno in a three-week period, failing to capitalise on his moment in the sun.

Gizzi did eventually fight for the British title, losing a close decision to Jack Bodell for the throne vacated by Cooper, and hung up his gloves in 1971 after losing the Welsh belt he had worn for six years.

Patterson boxed in Britain another five times, drawing once and losing to Billy Walker, Bodell, Joe Bugner and Richard Dunn. He retired in 1973 and still lives in Sweden.

41

★★★

EDDIE	vs.	MIKE
AVOTH		**QUARRY**

JUNE 6, 1970	Valley Music Theatre, Los Angeles

★★★

Eddie Avoth was used to being introduced to a crowd from the ring. But this was new. In the unfamiliar surroundings of a Welsh chapel in Los Angeles, the minister, a Swansea man, presented him to the congregation and the warmth of their applause informed him that he would not be without support when he took on local favourite Mike Quarry a few days later.

There was also encouragement from an unexpected source. While doing his roadwork in Griffith Park – itself named after an industrialist born at Bettws, near Bridgend – Avoth realised a police helicopter was circling overhead. It then swooped down and over its loudspeaker came the cry, "Good luck in the fight, Eddie!"

Both he and his opponent were from fighting families. The Avoths came from the no-frills Ely estate on the western fringe of Cardiff. The Quarry clan were raised in sunny California. In each case there were three boxing brothers. And they all looked for guidance to a father called Jack.

Mike Quarry had proved his abilities as an amateur even before turning pro a few weeks after his 18th birthday. Little more than a year later, he had 21 straight victories under his belt and was being mentioned as a possible challenger to world light-heavyweight king Bob Foster.

Eddie Avoth – born in Egypt, where Dad was stationed at the end of World War II – was six years older and had been paid for his punches since 1963. He won 20 out of 21 as a middleweight before rheumatic fever struck. Told he would never box again, the Welshman defied medical

Eddie Avoth

Mike Quarry

opinion, returning at light-heavy and claiming the British title in his new division.

Manager Eddie Thomas had his own designs on Foster – indeed, a match at Liverpool Stadium was already in the works - but considered Avoth would benefit from some transatlantic experience before tackling the brilliant champion from Albuquerque. He took his protégé to the west coast for two weeks' pre-fight preparation, with British-born film star Bob Hope among the celebrities who watched him in the gym. But Quarry was the man on familiar ground.

The pair came together in a theatre-in-the-round in the Los Angeles suburbs which had seen the likes of Sammy Davis, Jr, and Ray Charles strut their stuff and also hosted three of Mike's previous contests.

Urged on by his home crowd, Quarry took the action to Avoth from the start, but the Welshman's elegant left hand – typical of mentor Thomas and all his pupils – kept him at bay throughout the early stages. A few months earlier Eddie had injured his left shoulder falling from a horse and he was still hampered by the aftermath, unable to throw punches with his usual freedom. And, as the rounds went by, Mike's relentless aggression began to take its toll.

There were no knockdowns, but it was Quarry's forward movement, reinforced in three dominant closing sessions, which caught the judges' eyes and their verdict unanimously favoured the local man.

So it was Quarry who got to fight Foster, though it took another two years to achieve. By then Mike was 35-0, but it made no difference. Foster finished matters in four rounds.

He boxed on until 1982, but never had another shot. And he always looked back at the Avoth fight as his outstanding performance, insisting that the Welshman had forced him to a peak he was never to revisit.

Alas, Mike's later life, like that of heavyweight brother Jerry, was blighted by the effects of his ring wars, and he suffered from dementia for some years before his death in 2006, aged 55.

Avoth, his taste for travel unaffected by events in Los Angeles, headed for Australia to add the Commonwealth crown to his domestic honour. But both titles were taken from him by Olympic gold medallist Chris Finnegan – who would also defeat Quarry in London – and less than two years after his Californian adventure his gloves were locked away.

Eddie spent some time running a club in Spain, before returning to Wales and a number of businesses including property development and vehicle rental. He is still a regular and popular figure at boxing events.

42

★★★

JOHNNY	vs.	LUPE
OWEN		**PINTOR**

| **SEPTEMBER 19, 1980** | **Olympic Auditorium, Los Angeles** |

★★★

The Americans simply could not believe their eyes. Surely this skinny kid with the big ears was not really going to get in the ring with the teak-hard Mexican world champion?

Johnny Owen was used to it. A sympathetic supporter once said to his father-trainer, Dick, "You've got a lovely boy. But every time I see him I want to wrap him in a blanket, take him home and give him a big bowl of broth."

Other, more censorious voices castigated Dick and manager Dai Gardiner for allowing him to box, clearly unaware that the sport was Johnny's life. He kissed no girls, drank no beer, smoked no cigarettes. There was a tedious day job in a nut-and-bolt factory, but his free time was dedicated to training.

And when he climbed through the ropes, those who had seen no further than that bony exterior were soon made aware of a boundless determination to succeed. Deep wells of stamina, developed in daily runs across the Brecon Beacons above his Merthyr home, were complemented by fast hands and a tight defence.

They had brought Owen the bantamweight championships of Wales, Britain, Europe

Johnny Owen, the 'Merthyr Matchstick'

Lupe Pintor

and the Commonwealth. Only one target remained. Despite an initial reluctance to travel – Johnny's only loss had come in Spain, where local Juan Francisco Rodríguez had been allowed to indulge in a series of dubious activities en route to a majority decision – Gardiner took his charge to California to take on the WBC titleholder.

Nobody who saw José Guadalupe Pintor Guzmán questioned his suitability for his sport. The stocky, broad-shouldered product of the mean streets of Cuajimalpa, part of the urban sprawl that is Mexico City, learned to fight from an early age, having fled the fists of a violent father. He was still only 18 when he began doing it for money.

Pintor's early record was not perfect, but he was making waves. Within 18 months he was appearing in Los Angeles and rings across Texas, although few gave him much chance of dethroning his legendary countryman and stablemate, Carlos Zárate, when they collided at Caesars Palace in Las Vegas. The Z-Man was making his tenth defence and floored Lupe in the fourth round. One judge favoured Carlos by a massive 12 points; the others, incredibly, had Pintor one ahead.

Lupe's accession may have been controversial, but he had survived two defences – one a draw in Japan – before meeting Owen in front of a hugely pro-Mexican crowd, broken only by a couple of rows of travelling fans, who welcomed their hero as he walked to the ring behind the Welsh flag and a self-mocking banner depicting a skeleton with gloves on.

Pintor was 5-1 on, but the 'Merthyr Matchstick' ignored both that and the Hispanic hordes, forcing Lupe back in the early rounds. There were sporadic uppercuts to remind Johnny of his rival's threat, but the Mexican was the one showing the scars of battle, cuts over both eyes prompting referee Marty Denkin to check him out between sessions.

The official might have visited the challenger's corner, too. Owen was

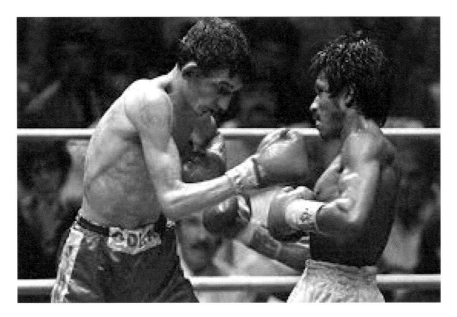

Owen gets home with a right

swallowing blood from a gash inside his lower lip, while each interval his seconds formed a barrier between him and Denkin's inquiring eyes. Ring doctor Bernhardt Schwarz spotted the problem, however, but, after a quick inspection, allowed the bout to proceed.

Pintor, always a slow starter, eventually realised that Johnny's constant pressure was not accompanied by power and began to walk through the Welshman's punches to land his own. The ninth marked the point at which a subtle change in the fight's course became clear-cut and decisive. A solid right rocked Owen, a follow-up left and right floored him for the first time in his life, amateur or pro.

He courageously saw out the round, but his usual self-belief had taken as damaging a blow as his jaw. The champion ruled the next two stanzas and the 12th brought the tragic climax. Decked by a short right, Johnny rose, wiping his nose with his glove, and nodded at the referee's inquiry as to his readiness to resume. Four punches later came the right hand which shattered Owen's world. He was unconscious before his head thudded into the canvas, fracturing his skull.

The jubilant crowd behaved appallingly, cheering the arrival of the stretcher. Others picked the pockets of the men bearing the motionless figure to a separate room and thence to an ambulance, which ferried the broken warrior to the nearby California Medical Center on the ironically

Johnny's father, Dick, hugs Pintor at the unveiling of his son's statue

named Hope Street. A three-hour operation to remove a blood clot failed to bring Johnny round. Seven weeks later, his distraught parents gave permission for the life-support machine to be switched off.

A post mortem revealed that the Welshman had an abnormally thin skull; what happened in Los Angeles could have occurred at any time. As a result of the discovery, the British Board of Control introduced compulsory brain scans. Today, Johnny would not be allowed a licence.

Pintor, urged by the Owen family to continue his career in their son's memory, made five further defences before abdicating to campaign at super-bantam. He ousted the brilliant Puerto Rican, Wilfredo Gómez, to capture a second WBC belt, which he wore for three years before losing it on the scales in Thailand. He returned after an eight-year lay-off, with mixed fortunes, and had passed 40 by the time he finally called it a day.

Financially secure, he opened a boxing school in Mexico City and, in November 2002, visited Merthyr, where he unveiled a statue commemorating his brave opponent. It was an occasion of mutual respect: a fighting community's welcome for the man whose fists had inadvertently robbed them of a favourite son, together with a boxer's desire to honour a former rival. Perhaps those so ready to condemn the sport should have been there.

43

★★★

COLIN		MILTON
JONES	**VS.**	**McCRORY**

MARCH 19, 1983	Convention Center, Reno

★★★

The publicists called him the 'Gorseinon Gravedigger'. It had a certain ring to it, even if Colin Jones's actual job with the local parks department involved more in the way of cutting grass and raking up leaves than wielding a spade. But he certainly left a string of early opponents metaphorically dead and buried.

Good enough as an amateur to compete in the Montreal Olympics at 17 – he lost to the eventual bronze medallist – his days in a vest came to a premature end, as with so many down the years, following a row with the Welsh ABA. Colin mislaid his team tracksuit at the European Championships, returning home to a bill for £40. He refused to pay and promptly turned pro with the Merthyr guru, Eddie Thomas.

Less than a fortnight after his 21st birthday, Jones won the British welterweight title, adding Commonwealth and European honours in due course. Just two days before he turned 24, the Swansea man was in Reno to challenge for the WBC belt vacated by Sugar Ray Leonard.

The man in the other corner was actually three years younger – and unbeaten. Milton McCrory, a product of the burgeoning Kronk academy in Detroit, had won a world junior title before joining the paid ranks as a teenager and halting his first 17 rivals. Coach Emanuel Steward had already piloted two Motown fighters to world crowns – Hilmer Kenty and Thomas Hearns – and the iconic gold trunks were becoming a familiar sight in boxing's highest circles.

McCrory, one of six children from a comfortably-off family on the city's East Side, was built to the Hearns model. More than six foot tall, he towered a good four

Colin Jones

Jones and McCrory could not be separated

inches above the stocky Welshman. Add some silky skills, honed in sparring sessions with Hall of Famer Hearns, plus home advantage and it was no surprise that the American was a clear favourite in the betting.

The original 6-1 against Jones was reduced to 3-1 by the first bell, thanks to the wagers of 100 or so travelling Welsh fans. The odds were still far too wide, although that was not immediately obvious, as Milton established his long left lead. But by the third – the session in which McCrory had promised a stoppage – Colin was beginning to land the occasional power punch and he returned to his corner with a grin towards the British press pack.

But it was still the American collecting the points. When Jones won his domestic honour against the supremely talented Kirkland Laing, he had been outboxed until landing the equaliser in the ninth; it seemed he was happy to wait for a similar scenario to play out.

The sixth saw Colin hurt 'The Iceman' with a rare left to the body and the following round saw McCrory looking increasingly tired as more and more Welsh ordnance began to get through. "I'd punched myself out after the eighth," confessed Milton later. "I hadn't known just how good he was."

Another body blow made the Kronk man grunt in discomfort and he took to his heels to avoid the ever-aggressive Jones. The change in tactic prompted boos from the Nevada crowd, who switched their backing to the Welsh invader. The travelling fans were also in fine voice: Colin's father, Raymond, employed by Welsh-language channel S4C to summarise alongside commentator John Evans, was so excited that he leapt up to encourage his boy and pulled the plugs out. But McCrory was still flicking out his left and scoring on the retreat, while Colin was tending to wait for a definitive single shot.

Promoter Don King was sufficiently concerned about his investment to spend the final stanza below the home corner, urging Milton to go for a strong finish. The American, his golden shorts stained with blood from his nose, dug deep and held his own until the final bell.

The first score to be announced was in favour of Jones, the second had McCrory ahead. The third, from Venezuelan Dimas Fernández, was 115-115. The WBC still had no champion. They had reduced the title-fight distance from 15 to 12 rounds following the death of Duk-Koo Kim the previous year; it is open to conjecture who would have benefited more had there been three more sessions. As it was, both camps thought they had won, although Colin lamented his failure to go downstairs earlier.

But the Swansea fighter, ever the businessman, was not too disheartened by the prospect of a rematch and another big cheque landing in his bank account. In that, at least, he would not be disappointed.

44

★★

COLIN
JONES

vs.

MILTON
McCRORY II

| AUGUST 13, 1983 | Dunes Hotel and Casino, Las Vegas |

★★

I f Colin Jones felt hard done by after his efforts in Reno – although most neutrals thought Milton McCrory the man with greater grounds for complaint – it was nothing to the anguish experienced by the Welshman when the duo met again. If anything, the rematch was even closer. And everything hinged on two knockdowns: one which happened, one which did not.

Following the draw, World Boxing Council president José Sulaimán ordered the pair to take 45 days to recover, after which there would be a 30-day period for the two camps to agree terms with the promoter of the first fight, his good friend Don King. If no deal could be made, the rematch would go out to purse offers.

That was not necessary. Eddie Thomas drove a hard bargain, but King was desperate to land what promised to be another classic and eventually came up with a remarkable £450,000 for Jones's services. This was a record payday for a British fighter and substantially more than the already impressive sum he had trousered for the first encounter.

But there was a downside. The 2.30 p.m. first bell would mean the BBC broadcasting at a sensible time for British viewers, but the heat of a summer afternoon in the desert was guaranteed to rise

Milton McCrory

Colin visits the canvas in the rematch

above 100 degrees Fahrenheit – without even considering the influence of the TV lights. In an attempt to acclimatise, Colin trained in Johnny Tocco's downtown sweatbox, while McCrory preferred the air-conditioned facilities of a converted ballroom at the Dunes, where both boxers stayed.

There were a few pre-fight problems. First there was a question mark over who actually owned the hotel. King was forced to bite the bullet, going without the usual "site fee" by which casinos attract big events, and paying rent for the 20,000-capacity outdoor arena erected in the car park; with a mere 2,000 turning up, Don took a financial bath. He attempted to recoup some of his losses by asking Colin to take a $100,000 cut in his purse, but the Welsh camp's lawyers put a stop to that.

Then Sulaimán, who occasionally seemed to make up the WBC rulebook as he went along, announced that if the scores were level again, the judges would be instructed to find a winner. The Nevada Commission felt that would put undue pressure on the officials. The Mexican backed down.

Jones was well aware that his slow start had contributed to his disappointment five months previously, but once again the lanky McCrory made the early pace. Colin had still to settle when, in the final moments of the opener, Milton curved a left uppercut between Jones's gloves and the Welshman fell to his hands and knees. He was aware enough to wink at Eddie Thomas, but needed the trainer's bluntness in the interval, when he complained he could not see.

"How the hell did you find your way back to the corner then?" asked Thomas, a response which jolted Colin into the realisation that he had to get on with things.

But it took at least three rounds for the Swansea man to recover fully from the knockdown. It was not until the fourth that Jones landed his feared left hook, but the success seemed to spur him on, with McCrory switching

Note the empty seats - promoter Don King lost a packet

to reverse gear. The fifth and sixth saw Colin jolt his man repeatedly, even beating him occasionally to the jab; there were hurtful blows to the body, an area so neglected in Reno, while Milton's nose began to leak a red stream that flowed for the rest of the contest.

The travelling support were in a ferment in the seventh as McCrory was sent reeling around the ring. One more clean punch would surely have dropped the American, but somehow he grabbed, hugged and stayed on his feet until the interval.

That minute's break proved decisive. It was not so much that McCrory was able to recuperate; more that Colin, worried about exhausting himself in the oven-like atmosphere, decided to slow down. As a result, the eighth, instead of supplying the exclamation mark in a demolition job, witnessed a stand-off which allowed the groggy Detroit fighter to regain his composure.

The ninth saw Colin land a big left hook which forced Milton to grab the top rope to maintain his balance and the Vegas crowd jeered their countryman as he clung on to avoid a repeat. Even a brief experiment with a southpaw stance did not help McCrory, who shipped a big right and reverted quickly to orthodox. Jones, his face wreathed in smiles, kept up the pressure and by the final session had surely wiped out any early-fight deficit.

McCrory must have been equally aware of the importance of the last three minutes. He reached beyond the pain and weariness to retrieve the last shreds of energy and determination, as both gladiators ignored the blistering heat to serve up a round to remember. At its conclusion, each was embraced by his cornermen and lifted shoulder-high in that gesture with which doubtful seconds attempt, too late, to influence wavering judges.

The Venezuelan judge looked way out of line with a four-point margin in McCrory's favour, his Panamanian colleague had Jones in front by one. The third arbiter, Mexican Rey Solís, also had just the single point between them – but he gave it to the American.

Colin was inconsolable. "How can he call himself a champion when he ran like a bloody thief?"

From the winning camp, the legendary Emanuel Steward forecast the rivalry could develop into an Ali-Frazier relationship. "They're so well matched they could fight five or six times and every one would be a thriller and there would never be a clear-cut winner," said the Kronk maestro. "But we don't even want to think about Jones for at least another year!"

In fact, the Welshman was never called on again throughout Milton's two-year reign, which ended in two painful rounds in a unification fight with WBA and IBF champion Don Curry. McCrory moved up to light-middle, losing a WBA challenge to Mike McCallum, and hung up his gloves in 1991. He worked for Chrysler for 15 years, occasionally calling in his old gym to pass on a few tips, but otherwise dropping off the boxing scene.

45

COLIN JONES

vs.

DON CURRY

| JANUARY 19, 1985 | National Exhibition Centre, Birmingham |

A n outstanding amateur who missed out on the Olympics due to the US boycott in Moscow, the 'Lone Star Cobra' had rampaged through the ranks as a professional.

His home town supporters in Fort Worth watched him outpoint unbeaten Korean Jun-Suk Hwang to claim the vacant WBA belt. Three months later big brother Bruce won the WBC light-welter strap, making them the first siblings to reign simultaneously. Don went further: the newly formed IBF proclaimed him their inaugural champion and three defences of the combined honours had taken his winning streak to 20.

Since his twin setbacks against McCrory, Jones had marked time with stoppage wins over two lesser Americans, Allen Braswell and Billy Parks, before Eddie Thomas gave him the news for which he was waiting. Not only was he getting a shot at the other two titles (not that anyone in the UK acknowledged the IBF's existence at the time), but Curry was willing to cross the Atlantic.

Both completed their preparation at the Lynch brothers' gym in Birmingham, but at separate times. Jones was annoyed by a comment Curry made on arrival in Britain which suggested he was unaware that Wales was a separate country; Thomas cautiously kept them apart, turning down invitations

Don Curry

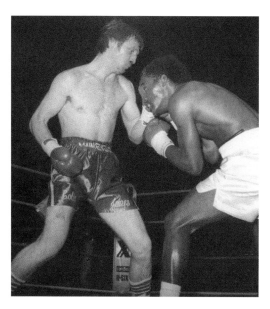

Jones enjoys a rare success

for joint appearances in radio and TV studios.

Snow was piled alongside the motorways as fans headed for the Midlands, but there was still optimism that the old saying - "Three tries for a Welshman" – would prove true in the case of the man from Gorseinon. Insiders were less sanguine; the trade paper, *Boxing News*, had just pronounced Curry their Overseas Boxer of the Year for 1984.

At 23, the Texan was the shooting star, the silky-skilled prodigy who was emerging from the long shadow of predecessor Ray Leonard. Jones was only 25, but had been a pro for eight years and had looked less than scintillating in dealing with the ordinary Parks seven months earlier.

That encounter, at the Afan Lido, had also seen the Welshman cut near the right eye, the first serious such injury of his career. It left him concerned about a possible repeat.

"It must be terrible for any fighter whose title chance is destroyed in that way," he said in the days before the contest. "I know I'd be heartbroken if it happened to me on Saturday."

Lax stewarding allowed well-wishers to belabour Colin with backslaps all the way to the ring, where he was welcomed by a grinning Curry acolyte offering him the WBA belt, saying, "Do you want it now?" The challenger's nerves were not helped by a lengthy delay to accommodate American television and when the bell finally sounded it was soon followed by a series of jabs in Jones's face and a right which made the recipient lurch sideways.

Even one of Colin's trademark lefts to the body brought no change in Curry's impassive features, while the champion's right gave the Welshman a nosebleed to take back to his stool. The second saw Don maintain the pressure in a bout fought almost exclusively at short range, the pair having seemingly decided that there was little to be gained from reconnaissance missions.

Jones battled back, hooking with both hands, to bring the 11,500 sell-out crowd – the first million-pound gate in British history - to their feet, and he started the third with a similar assault. But disaster was only seconds away. Curry launched his most sustained attack so far and Colin's face and body were suddenly scarlet; when he turned at the gong, even those at the back of the hall could see the gash across the bridge of the prominent Jones nose. Those closer realised the game was up there and then.

Even Eddie Thomas, that wizard of the swabstick whose talents had famously helped Ken Buchanan to a world crown, could not stem the flow. The first punch of the fourth renewed the torrent and when referee 'Wiso' Fernández took Jones to the ropes for a doctor's examination, there could be only one outcome. Tears mingled with the blood as Colin bent over in despair.

As the official announcements were made, Jones looked wistfully at Curry's belt. As if acknowledging that his last chance to own one had gone, the Welshman bent forward and kissed it. As the winner paraded the ring in a theatre-prop crown, he allowed Colin to wear it briefly, a rueful grin on his battered face.

Curry lets Colin borrow his crown

By the end of the year Curry had confirmed his overall superiority by demolishing WBC boss McCrory in two rounds. But he was beginning to struggle with the scales and Londoner Lloyd Honeyghan snatched his three belts in a mighty upset in Atlantic City.

Don promptly stepped up to light-middleweight and, although Mike McCallum repelled a challenge for the WBA throne, the WBC strap went back to Texas after Curry floored Gianfranco Rosi five times in his native Italy. He lost it in another odds-defying result, outpointed in France by René Jacquot, and failure in two further world title tilts, against Michael Nunn – at middle – and Terry Norris, saw the 'Cobra' call it a day.

Don became a trainer, but in 1994 was arrested with two other former boxers on drug-smuggling charges. He was eventually acquitted on all counts, but fighting the case had eaten deep into his bank balance and he was jailed for failing to pay child support. The need for cash forced him into an unwise comeback, but, after a sustained beating from former pupil Emmett Linton, he retired for good.

For Jones, there were no more punches to be thrown, but at least there was financial security, having invested his money in a building firm and other business interests. But there was no break from boxing: he was soon passing on his knowledge to a new generation, first taking over his old Penyrheol amateur club and, in 2010, becoming national coach to the Welsh ABA.

46

★★★

FLOYD
HAVARD

VS.

'JOHN-JOHN'
MOLINA

| JANUARY 22, 1994 | Welsh Institute of Sport, Cardiff |

★★★

The champion was getting impatient. "Can I knock him out next round?" he kept asking in heavily accented English.

Each time his craggy old trainer urged him to wait. "This guy is fighting before his own people," came the reply. "Let him put on a show for a while."

Then, after five rounds had passed, Lou Duva relented. "OK," he told 'John-John' Molina, "Get it over with!"

At the end of the next session, the pair were celebrating victory.

In fairness, the odds had been against Floyd Havard from the moment the match was made. The 28-year-old southpaw from the Swansea Valley village of Craigcefnparc had indeed worn the British super-feather crown, having dethroned the world-class, if ageing Pat Cowdell, but recurrent problems with both hands had flared up in his first defence against Yorkshireman John Doherty, prompting him to retire after 11 rounds.

Despite surgery to graft bone from a hip on to the troublesome knuckles, his right went again two years later and, although he was on a five-bout winning streak following the title loss, injuries meant he had boxed

Floyd Havard

only twice in the previous two years. Tackling 'John-John' was a big ask.

Having represented his native Puerto Rico at the 1984 Los Angeles Olympics, Juan Molina Cruz had based himself in the States for most of his professional career. He was in his second reign as IBF champion and had also ruled the 9st 4lb (130lb) division with the WBO. His last two defences had seen him outpoint former world feather boss Manuel Medina and halt Bernard Taylor, who had drawn in previous championship action.

Where Floyd's 12-round experience was confined to those two domestic title fights, his rival, only seven months older, had been in 10, all at the highest level. And, as if he needed any further handicaps, the Welshman suffered a broken nose in the later stages of preparation.

At the pre-fight press conference, promoter Frank Maloney suggested, optimistically, that 2,000 Welshmen would sing his man home. Duva, a grin splitting a face that looked as if it had been carved by those responsible for the presidential heads on Mount Rushmore, suggested *Show Me The Way To Go Home*. Havard preferred *Another One Bites The Dust*.

'John-John' with trainer Lou Duva

All good knockabout stuff. But come the first bell, only one man was doing the knocking about. And it wasn't Floyd.

The West Walian started confidently, finding his range with a fluency that belied his lack of recent activity. But Molina stepped up the pace in the second and maintained it with ease, forcing Havard to focus almost exclusively on warding off the torrent of blows heading in his direction.

'John-John' brushed aside Floyd's defensive right leads and in the third a stunning right of his own prompted the challenger to take a pace back and go down on one knee in search of respite. Molina's enthusiasm saw him hurl a couple of supplementary punches while Havard was still down, but Florida referee Brian Garry let it ride.

With the cautious and charitable Duva urging patience, the Puerto Rican was less headstrong, but just as effective, in the sessions which followed. By the sixth, Floyd was bleeding steadily, his fragile nose fractured once more, while an ugly bruise beneath his left eye was swelling ominously. A brief knockdown underlined the inevitability of defeat and the bell brought a sensible withdrawal from the fray.

Mirror image as Molina and Havard clash

The emphatic nature of the loss might have spelt the end for some fighters. Not Havard: just two months later he halted fellow-Welshman Neil Haddock to regain his British crown. He defended it twice before relinquishing and, in fact, won all six post-Molina contests before disappearing in 1996.

There was sporadic talk of comebacks, but nothing concrete until a brief venture into the unlicensed ring at the age of 44, when, by now a light-welter, he beat a 40-year-old for another so-called "British title".

As well as security work – he looked after Robbie Williams and the Spice Girls among others – Floyd has dabbled in several fields, including a period training boxers in the Ukraine.

Molina, meanwhile, completed seven defences before moving up to lightweight, only for world title attempts to fall short against hall-of-famers Oscar de la Hoya and Shane Mosley. He slimmed back to super-feather, but hopes of a third reign were dashed by Roberto Garcia. And, although he continued until he was 36, that was that at the top level.

47

NICKY
vs.
PIPER

LEEONZER
BARBER

JANUARY 29, 1994	National Ice Rink, Cardiff

★★

The two men came from very different backgrounds, but produced a thriller which was settled by a single punch. And it left the hometown fighter forever doomed to reflect on how near he had come to a world crown.

Nicky Piper was an articulate youngster from the Culverhouse Cross area of Cardiff who followed five Welsh schoolboy titles with four at senior level, covering three weight divisions. Finally, after winning the British ABA title on his 23rd birthday, he opted to turn pro with Frank Warren, while trained by his mentor at the Penarth amateur club, Charlie Pearson. Unusually, he remained loyal to both men throughout his career.

For Leeonzer Barber, life was a struggle from the start. Brought up in a rough area of Detroit, he was introduced to the ring after an embarrassing encounter with a neighbour.

He was just five and she was nine – "and a big nine," insists Barber – and she kept pushing him over in his own backyard. His mother, who saw it all through the kitchen window, insisted that his father, who boxed a bit, should take him to the gym and teach him to defend himself.

Young Leeonzer preferred kung fu, reckoning that it must be better if you can use your feet as well, but when he lost to a boxer he was convinced that the orthodox code was the way to go. A pro at 20, his early career was a stop-start affair, with

Nicky Piper

The Welshman on the attack

managerial problems and a spell in the Marines delaying his progress.

For Piper things went more smoothly. An IQ of 153 and membership of the bright sparks' club, Mensa, earned him nationwide publicity and TV coverage, while his punching power – two of his first bouts ended inside 20 seconds – underlined that he had more than a gimmick to support him.

A rash gamble saw him stopped by the much heavier Carl Thompson, later to become WBO cruiser king, and prompted a drop to super-middle, where he was handed a shot at fearsome WBC ruler Nigel Benn and surprised many, leading on one card when Benn finally brought down the curtain in the 11th.

By then Barber was wearing the WBO light-heavy belt. He showed rapid improvement after impressing legendary trainer Emanuel Steward and taking his place in the world-renowned Kronk gym. British fans saw his ability for themselves when he travelled to Leeds to halt Yorkshireman Tom Collins for the vacant title.

His first three defences went the full course, however, and Nicky noted that the American tired late on against Italian Andrea Magi. It led to a stand-off over the weigh-in time when the pair came together in Cardiff. WBO rules called for the men to mount the scales at lunchtime on the day of the fight, but allowed for the ceremony to take place the previous evening if both agreed.

Barber wanted the early time, but Piper refused and the holder had to stay below the limit until a few hours before the first bell. In the event, it mattered little.

Nicky came out with uncharacteristic aggression, forcing the pace, and by the end of the opener his trademark left hook had produced an ugly bruise alongside the American's right eye. As it swelled, it impeded Barber's vision and the challenger was able to land the punch repeatedly.

Leeonzer showed all the ringcraft associated with the Kronk academy, however, and landed his share, with no sign of the weight-making weariness hoped for by the Welshman. But Piper gradually took control, urged on by the 2,000-plus crowd, and was confident enough to wink at the fans during a clinch in the eighth.

Barber with the eye damage that nearly cost him his title

The champion's camp saw the way things were going. With Barber's eye now almost closed, veteran cornerman Luther Burgess – Steward was in Las Vegas with Thomas Hearns – told him he would pull him out after the next session. It never came to that.

Nicky, unaware of the ultimatum, kept pressing for the stoppage. Momentarily, he lost focus and his hands dropped slightly. Barber threw a desperate left hook and it landed flush; Piper wobbled, then crashed on to his back. Somehow he dragged himself upright before the completion of referee Ismael Quiñones's count, but one more right hand was enough to send him down for keeps.

"I did lose concentration, because I was getting tired," admits Nicky, who had certainly earned his conqueror's respect. "He's got a little juice in that hook and he was sure boxing like he had some soul," acknowledged Barber.

Piper was to have one more crack at the world title, going down in seven rounds in Germany to the unbeaten Pole, Dariusz Michalczewski, who had dethroned Barber. He hung up the gloves and has served the Board of Control, first as an administrative steward and now as marketing consultant.

Barber, after losing his crown, made a couple of abortive comebacks before finally calling it a day in 2004.

48

★★★

ROBBIE
VS.
DANIEL
REGAN
JIMÉNEZ

| APRIL 26, 1996 | Welsh Institute of Sport, Cardiff |

★★★

It was the second time the Welshman had tried for a world title. And once again he found himself up against someone called Jiménez. The first had ended painfully, Robbie Regan's wife unable to watch as he writhed in agony on a table in a sparsely-furnished room at the National Ice Rink while fight doctor Ray Monsell scraped clean a deep gash between his knuckles.

Robbie Regan, with Dai Gardiner (left) and uncle Pat Chidgey

Earlier, up the stairs in an arena where the ice sent chilly waves through the temporary covering, the Blackwood boy had been a brave, but distant second to Mexican hard man Alberto Jiménez until trainer Dai Gardiner pulled his man out after nine painful rounds. As well as the recurrence of the hand damage that had earlier prompted a three-week postponement, Regan needed eight stitches in a cut above his left eye.

The little warrior from the Gwent Valleys had been with Gardiner since he first laced on a glove. The trim-bearded trainer had abandoned the sport in the wake of Johnny Owen's death, but then resolved to return and seek a fighter who could claim the world honours that so tragically eluded the 'Merthyr Matchstick'. In Regan, he felt he had found him.

Amateur success was quickly followed

by pro laurels, with Welsh, British and European belts marking his ascent. If the first Jiménez on his record had proved too strong, it merely inspired Robbie to redouble his efforts.

Three months later he thought he had achieved his goal, halting Tunisian southpaw Ferid ben Jeddou in two to become the IBF interim titleholder. Or so he – and everyone at the Sophia Gardens venue – believed. Then the New Jersey-based organisation changed their mind and denied they had approved the bout – though they never returned the sanctioning fee!

The frustrated Welshman (and furious promoter Frank Warren) turned back to the WBO, Regan stepping up a weight to tackle a second Jiménez. Daniel had done it in reverse; having dethroned Duke McKenzie in London to win the WBO super-bantam crown, he retained it four times – including a record 17-second demolition of Harald Geier in Austria – before being ousted by the brilliant Marco Antonio Barrera.

Daniel Jiménez

Puerto Rican Jiménez, a former university student now a recreational leader in his home town of Camuy, dropped four pounds and returned to London to edge out Ghanaian Alfred Kotey and collect his second WBO strap at bantam. He then outscored Scot Drew Docherty in an unimpressive first defence, but his run of success on British soil had most pundits expecting a repeat.

Jiménez, who blamed his sluggish showing against Docherty on a spot of Christmas over-indulgence and the resultant struggle to shed the surplus, surprised the Welsh camp with his early sharpness. Gardiner had instructed Regan to move in and out, working off the jab, but Daniel more than matched him in that area and Robbie's face was soon marking up.

The challenger changed tack in the fourth, urged to stay close and apply pressure. Gradually, he began to slow Jiménez to the extent that Regan's left hooks were finding the target. One such blow in the seventh saw spray flying from the Puerto Rican's head; another, late in the eighth, dropped the champion.

Jiménez lands a left, but loses his crown

Daniel rose at three, realised his legs were unsteady and dropped to his haunches for another five seconds of referee Geno Rodriguez's count. The bell prevented any follow-up, but Robbie was now glowing with confidence. Despite swallowing blood for the final sessions after a mouth ulcer burst, Regan landed solidly, while blocking Jiménez's replies with his gloves.

The three judges were unanimous. The trio, from Holland, Canada and Luxembourg, had margins of two, three and five points. But it was only when MC Mike Goodall reached the words "the NEW" that Wales could be sure it had its sixth world champion. The crowd's response drowned the rest of Goodall's announcement; the new monarch himself was in tears, just as at the end of that showdown with the other Jiménez, but this time it was through pure joy.

The visitor was a sporting loser, but an unhappy one. "When he landed, the crowd went wild," he pointed out. "When I did, silence. These things influence the judges." A case of Daniel in the Dragon's Den...

He did get one more, unsuccessful shot at a title in a career that still had six years to run. Regan, though he did not realise it, would never box again.

The first blow came with a kidney ailment, the Epstein-Barr virus, which meant the repeated postponement of dates with Docherty and a new interim champion, Jorge Eliécer Julio. Finally, 21 months after winning the belt, Regan had overcome the infection; Colombian Julio arrived in Cardiff to have his belated opportunity.

The pair even came face-to-face for the traditional pre-fight press conference. But as he left the building, Gardiner's phone rang. It was an official of the Board of Control. Robbie had failed his brain scan.

Despite a desperate dash to London for a second opinion, there was no reprieve. Two nights later, the distraught Welshman climbed through the ropes at Cardiff International Arena to make it official: the Robbie Regan story was at an end.

49

★★

JOE		OMAR
CALZAGHE	**vs.**	**SHEIKA**

| **AUGUST 12, 2000** | **Wembley Conference Centre, London** |

★★

As an undefeated world champion with five successful defences to his name, Joe Calzaghe should have been a happy man. But he had been given little credit for his achievements, particularly by pundits in the States.

Recurrent injuries to his hands and an elbow had hampered the Newbridge southpaw's training to the extent that he frequently entered the ring without a single round's sparring. Small wonder he was no longer knocking opponents out with the ease that had seen him convert his amateur success – the first man since the 1920s to win three successive British ABA titles at different weights – into, first, the British super-middle crown and then, flooring and outpointing the formidable Chris Eubank, the vacant WBO super-middle throne.

But recent sluggish performances had seen a split-decision win over former WBC king Robin Reid followed by distance fights against unambitious rivals Rick Thornberry and David Starie. There was pressure from unhappy promoter Frank Warren for Calzaghe to drop his Sardinian-born father, Enzo, as his trainer, while sceptical Americans were sure that the first half-

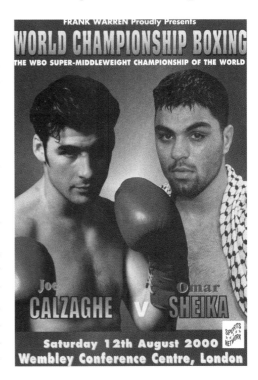

Joe Calzaghe

decent Yank to face him would end his reign.

That was certainly Omar Sheika's opinion – and the New Jersey man considered himself a lot better than half-decent. Perhaps a controversial points loss to Yorkshire journeyman Tony Booth two years earlier suggested otherwise, but that was the only blot on his 21-fight record and he had stopped unbeaten Londoner Toks Owoh on the undercard of Joe's defence against Paraguayan Juan Carlos Giménez in Cardiff. In addition, his last two bouts had seen Omar outpoint former world champion Simon Brown and perennial contender Glen Johnson.

As a result, there was no lack of noise when Sheika and his substantial entourage landed in Britain. His antics on arrival – punching holes in posters, telling Calzaghe he was "going to kill him" and the like – focussed Joe's mind perfectly, while abandoning the local pitch-and-putt course seemed to have solved the elbow problem. The old confidence was back and it showed from the first bell.

The champion's speed and southpaw stance confused Sheika from the start and he found it difficult to ward off the blows coming his way, let alone respond with anything meaningful of his own. The visitor enjoyed some success midway through the second, but Calzaghe looked unworried, even having the better of the close exchanges, expected to be Omar's territory.

The Palestinian-American paid aggressive attention to Joe's body, but it was a tactic that meant heads were beginning to come together and late in the fourth one such collision brought blood pouring from Sheika's left eyebrow. He complained to Chicago referee Geno Rodriguez in the interval, but was firmly informed that the clash had been his own fault.

There was a touch of desperation about Omar's approach to the fifth and Calzaghe met him toe-to-toe. Another cut appeared over the challenger's right eye and the third man halted the action to inspect the damage before waving them back in. Sheika's defence was now in shreds and when he staggered under a barrage of head shots, Mr Rodriguez leapt to the rescue.

The MC's announcement that cuts had brought about the finish appeared to provide the unhappy Sheika with an excuse to take home, but it was incorrect. Asked if the injuries had prompted his intervention, Mr Rodriguez was adamant. "Not so," he said. "I stopped it because he was getting beat up!"

Still only 23, Omar headed home insistent that his time would come. It never did. There were three more world title shots, but Eric Lucas, Jeff Lacy and Markus Beyer each outpointed him, while others – Thomas Tate, Scott Pemberton and Roy Jones, Jr - needed no help from the judges.

For Calzaghe, however, the emphatic manner of the victory brought redemption. The British press, who had grown increasingly critical, agreed that the old Joe was back. And armchair fans in the US, having snored through the Starie maul, finally saw what the fuss was about.

Omar Sheika

50

★★★

JOE
CALZAGHE
VS.

CHARLES
BREWER

| APRIL 20, 2002 | Cardiff International Arena |

★★★

T he murmurs began to increase in volume. Those vultures temporarily mollified by the Welshman's disposal of Omar Sheika were circling once more. And again the barbs focussed on the standard of his challengers.

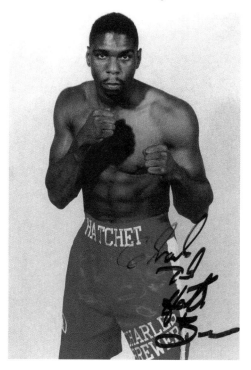

Charles Brewer

While they were harsh when it came to friend and rival Richie Woodhall, who, after all, had worn the WBC belt, they could not easily be rebutted as far as Calzaghe's two most recent foes were concerned. Neither Mario Veit nor Will McIntyre were worthy of world title shots – but it was hardly fair to blame Joe for their appearance in the opposite corner.

Veit, the German despatched inside a round, had won all 30 contests, yet had no business occupying the No 1 spot in the WBO rankings; but there he was, and Calzaghe had to face him or risk being stripped. American McIntyre was even worse – although he lasted three rounds longer - but was only called up after both Antwun Echols and Hassine Cherifi had declined the job.

There could be no complaints regarding Joe's next opponent, however. Charles Brewer, a 32-year-old computer programmer from Philadelphia with a bullet embedded in his chest, had worn the IBF crown with honour, his three unsuccessful challengers including classy Englishman Herol Graham, like Calzaghe a southpaw, and when he was dethroned by three-time Olympian Sven Ottke in Germany, one of the judges gave it to Brewer by six points. A rematch produced another controversial split-decision success for the local.

There had since been a stoppage loss to the reluctant Echols, but Charles went on to acquire the vacant North American title with a clear verdict over tough Ecuadorian Fernando Zúñiga. 'The Hatchet' was fully expected to give Joe a real test. The man himself anticipated more, dismissing Calzaghe as "just another average, straight-up European fighter".

The bout was originally planned as the Welshman's US debut, but with all Showtime's production teams tied up at the Winter Olympics in Salt Lake City, it had to be switched to Cardiff, though still broadcast in the States. And those viewers tearing themselves away from the figure-skating had a feast to relish.

Within the first minute the Welsh crowd were roaring as their man stood toe-to-toe with the challenger, pummelling the body, although Brewer's occasional success to the head ensured the exchanges were fully competitive.

It was a pattern followed throughout 12 thrilling rounds. While the normally light-hitting Graham, a ringside observer, had floored Brewer

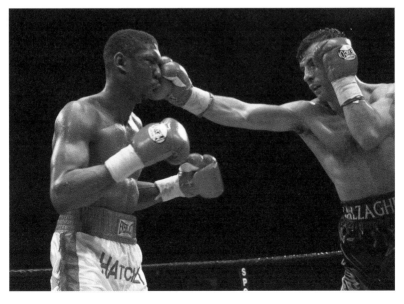

Calzaghe lands a right ...

... and his left is equally effective

twice en route to his defeat, Joe was never able to budge him. But Charles found the champion's chin equally resilient as the pair maintained a hectic pace.

In the seventh, Brewer hurt Calzaghe both to head and body, but Joe, his ears bruised by a high-decibel rant from father-trainer Enzo in the interval, came through his sticky patch and used his speed and footwork to stay clear of too much trouble in the closing stretch. There was a final close-quarter set-to to cap an enthralling contest, but there was little doubt about the outcome.

While Ottke may have benefitted from a little "home cooking" against Brewer – it was hardly surprising that every one of Sven's 22 world title fights took place in Germany – there were no complaints from the American camp when Calzaghe was voted in by five, seven and 10 points, especially as the widest margin came from American judge Chuck Giampa.

Brewer worked his way back into championship contention, but stoppage defeats by Veit and Kinshasa-born Dane Lolenga Mock convinced him that it was time to seek a quieter life.

51

JOE CALZAGHE vs. BYRON MITCHELL

| JUNE 28, 2003 | Cardiff International Arena |

This was not in the script. Joe Calzaghe was on a roll against Americans. This was his fifth successive opponent from across the Atlantic and fully expected to go the same way as Will McIntyre, Charles Brewer, Miguel Jimenez and Tocker Pudwill. But Byron Mitchell had other ideas.

And he had put them into effect. A short upward right early in the second round had sent the Welshman to the canvas for the first time in his life, amateur or professional. This time he was in a real fight.

Not that he had ever doubted it. Byron Deangelo-Tarone Mitchell, more commonly, if less impressively, known as the "Slamma From 'Bama", had pedigree. Twice he had worn the WBA super-middle strap, most recently losing it in similar fashion to IBF counterpart Brewer, going down via split decision in Germany to Sven Ottke in a clash which saw one judge favour the American by four points.

That had happened just three months earlier. As a result Mitchell, whose first title loss had been to Bruno Girard in Paris, was determined not to leave matters to the opinions of others. And he had proven power: in both his belt-winning battles, against Frankie Liles – a southpaw, like Calzaghe - and Manny Siaca, the man from Ozark, Alabama, had been way behind on the cards when he found the punches to force a stoppage late on.

Pre-fight comments from the American camp suggested they felt Joe's come-forward style would play into Byron's hands. And the Newbridge fighter was certainly bent on attack, taking out his frustration at the political machinations which had kept him inactive for six

Byron Mitchell

The end is nigh for the challenger

months, with William Joppy the latest big name to turn him down. Even the Mitchell date had been put back three times.

After a few exploratory forays, Calzaghe seemed to convince himself there was little to worry about and began to unload. Two left hooks jolted Mitchell's shaven skull and the challenger looked flustered under the relentless pressure. Joe increased the pace in the second and rocked his man with a right, but this time Byron gritted his teeth and hurled leather back.

A couple of body shots brought a grimace from the champion, who momentarily left himself square-on as he tried to reply. Then came the punch that spun him around and sent him to his knees. The 5,000 crowd were stunned; happily, Joe was not and quickly regained his feet to take the mandatory eight-count.

Scorning defence, he stormed into Mitchell, the pair trading toe-to-toe as the delirious ringsiders screamed their encouragement. As Byron tried to force Calzaghe back, he shipped a thumping left to the jaw that sent him crashing, his head through the ropes, though he, too, rose immediately.

With a minute left in the session, Joe went for the kill. No fewer than 20 unanswered blows poured in as the bewildered American back-pedalled frantically. He did not appear unduly hurt, but was throwing nothing in return and when he stumbled backwards into the ropes, referee Dave Parris jumped in and signalled that he had seen enough.

Mitchell looked mildly surprised, but acquiescent. The intervention may have been marginally premature, but few felt that any great wrong had occurred. The better man had prevailed.

The American did not box again for another four years and when he finally laced on the gloves, he lacked his old resilience. He was halted in eight of his dozen remaining contests, as a series of prospects added a faded champion's name to their records. Joe Calzaghe had, in effect, destroyed Byron Mitchell as a top-class fighter.

52

I f anyone doubted the fighting credentials of the part-time actor and model from Massachusetts when he climbed through the ropes to challenge for the WBU cruiserweight belt, a glance at his corner should have satisfied them. Alongside Richie LaMontagne stood an 81-year-old man with boxing history in his veins.

Goody Petronelli, with brother Pat - childhood friends of Rocky Marciano - had guided the career of the legendary Marvin Hagler, while their gym in Brockton, Massachusetts, also saw the professional development of Dubliner Steve Collins.

And there had been a time when Goody fancied that 'The Mountain' might reach the same heights. He certainly had the punch: after turning pro in 1993, he had disposed of nine of his first 14 opponents in less than a round. As the standard of his rivals improved, the job took longer, but he still extended his unbeaten run to 20 contests,

But world title contenders such as Kenny Keane and Vasiliy Jirov outpointed him – though he was the first to last the course with future IBF ruler Jirov - and, while he went on to knock out the likes of Sydney Olympian Michael Bennett, it was clear that Richie was never to reach the very top. There were a few minor belts to take home, though, and his trip to Wales was an opportunity to add another.

Enzo Maccarinelli, like his friend Joe Calzaghe,

Enzo Maccarinelli

133

LaMontagne comes under fire

had an Italian father. Mario, a former Army boxer from Brescia, moved to Wales in 1954 to work down the pit. He settled in Swansea and raised a family, passing on his ring knowledge to the boys.

With his Bonymaen club on the rebel side of a split which crippled Welsh amateur boxing in the 1990s, Enzo was unable to represent his country internationally, so turned pro shortly after his 19th birthday. Although an early knockout by journeyman Lee Swaby raised the first questions over the young man's chin, it was usually the other guy having to be carried back to his corner.

Guided by Charlie Pearson, the veteran Cardiffian who had looked after Nicky Piper, Maccarinelli soon moved into title contention and acquired the WBU strap by halting Londoner Bruce Scott – although he had to survive a torrid first round to do so. There followed five successful defences before the arrival of LaMontagne.

At 35 – 11 years older than the Welshman – pre-fight debate concerned how much LaMontagne had left. Not enough, it transpired. The pattern was set early on when a series of solid lefts from Enzo removed the confident smile from the visitor's face. Twice he subsided following close-quarter exchanges; the first time referee Dave Parris considered it a slip, the second brought a count.

Although LaMontagne tried to battle back, he shipped a left and right as the bell rang to finish the opener, staggering backwards before falling and having to undergo the mandatory eight before he was allowed to seek respite on his stool.

A patient Maccarinelli waited for an opening and when it came, with another knockdown at the end of the second, the gong once again rescued Richie. Somehow the American survived the third, escaping another count when Mr Parris missed a glove touching the canvas, but time was running out.

When two more lefts buckled LaMontagne's knees after a minute of the fourth, the referee jumped between them. Richie pulled away and pleaded with Enzo to carry on regardless, while his brother, Steve, whose brain should have been working more clearly, upbraided the third man for calling a halt. The venerable Goody, however, nodded to himself.

He, at least, realised that his brave pupil had reached the end of the road. In time, LaMontagne agreed. He never boxed again.

Maccarinelli, however, moved on to bigger things, defending his WBU title once more before trading it in for the more prestigious WBO version.

53

JOE CALZAGHE vs. JEFF LACY

MARCH 4, 2006	MEN Arena, Manchester

Joe Calzaghe had been world champion for seven and a half years. He had won all 40 fights as a professional, including 17 defences of his WBO super-middleweight belt. Among those unsuccessful challengers were six Americans, two of them former titleholders. Yet still the Yanks refused to acknowledge his quality.

And now they had the man they were certain would prove their point. Jeff 'Left Hook' Lacy had been an outstanding amateur, with the 2000 Olympics on his CV, and he had transferred that ability seamlessly into the paid ranks.

Calzaghe and Lacy meet before the fight

The "next American superstar" is already in trouble

Four first-round victories to open his account testified to his power. He began to accumulate a few regional honours and his world supremacy seemed inevitable. He duly captured the vacant IBF super-middle strap in his 18th bout, halting Canadian Syd Vanderpool, and retained it four times, though two of his victims, Omar Sheika and Robin Reid, had been seen off by Calzaghe several years earlier.

The hype machine was moving into overdrive. Lacy was "the next Mike Tyson", the man who would single-handedly revive the flagging US fight scene. And the young man from St Petersburg, Florida, would take the step to superstardom by seeing off the "slapper" from Newbridge.

Jeff, perhaps paying Calzaghe the respect denied him by some of his compatriots, regarded the Welshman as the prize scalp that would guarantee his pound-for-pound status – and he was willing to cross the Atlantic to meet him. The match was made for November 2005, but Calzaghe rashly opted for a warm-up against Kenyan Evans Ashira. The champion took every round on all three cards – but broke his left hand on the African's head. The "career-defining fight" he had craved for so long was off.

There were the inevitable jibes from the sceptics, but both camps – and, vitally, US television giants Showtime – were determined the unification bout should go ahead. Eventually, they settled on a 2.30 a.m. start in Manchester, allowing Lacy, in Britain for two weeks before the fight, to keep his watch on Florida time.

Calzaghe was 34, Lacy 28. After a series of less than stellar displays, Joe was perceived as a fighter in decline. Jeff was the coming man, whose demolition job on the faded Reid had impressed many in Britain, to the extent that even the home bookies had the American as a 10-11 favourite.

Reid himself, and their other mutual foe, Sheika, were backing Lacy. Even the trade paper, *Boxing News*, tipped the visitor. Rarely have pundits and punters been so wrong.

Their misjudgment was clear from the first bell. Within the early exchanges, both had landed cleanly: Calzaghe walked through Lacy's shots, while his own brought blood streaming from the other man's nose. It was a pattern that varied little as the Welshman served up an exhibition few have ever equalled.

The speed and volume of Joe's blows, allied to his mobility, had Jeff befuddled. When the IBF champion tried to come in low, he was straightened up by vicious uppercuts. When he moved forward in more orthodox fashion, there were lightning combinations to greet him.

If Lacy wanted to box, Calzaghe outskilled him; if he hurled punches at

close range, he found Joe willing to trade. By the end of the fourth, the American was leaking red from damage over both eyes. The 12,000 crowd chanted, "Easy, easy!" – and for once, it was no exaggeration.

Only dogged courage kept Lacy on his feet. Many corners might have pulled him out, acknowledging the Welshman's superiority and saving their man for another day. At one stage voluble manager Gary Shaw seemed to be suggesting as much, but Dan Birmingham, recently voted US Trainer of the Year, ignored his signals.

In the penultimate session, Joe had Jeff's head trapped beneath his right arm and cheekily threw a token left behind his back. It barely landed, but referee Raul Caiz opted to take a point from him – the only thing which prevented a whitewash on the cards.

While many would have settled for a virtual lap of honour in the last, Calzaghe wanted more. He ripped into the battered Lacy, who finally dropped to the canvas. He rose bravely at four for the mandatory count and held on desperately for the remainder of the round.

Two of the judges scored it 119-107, the third went for 119-105. But the figures could only hint at the masterclass that had gone before. And, finally, even the Americans recognised Joe's greatness.

"I haven't seen a better performance by any boxer for many, many

Joe celebrates during the last round

years," acknowledged the chastened Birmingham, while across the ocean pound-for-pound leader Floyd Mayweather conceded, "Calzaghe ain't nothing but the truth. Joe has some serious skills – and it takes a lot to impress me."

Only after the dust had settled did Joe reveal that three weeks earlier he had been on the verge of pulling out. A wrist injury had left him unable to spar and his first instinct was to cry off rather than face the formidable Lacy while less than 100 per cent. On the train home after seeing a Harley Street specialist, he phoned his father, but for once Enzo did not support his decision.

He let his son know, in no uncertain terms, that withdrawal would see the end, not just of the Lacy fight, but any talk of scraps with the likes of Bernard Hopkins or Roy Jones, Jr. For all his achievements, Joe would be remembered as 'Sicknote', castigated as "chicken" for the rest of his life.

Stunned by the anger in his father's voice – coupled with his insistence that Lacy was "made for you" – he went through with the engagement. And made history.

History, too, for the American. His painful humiliation effectively finished him as a top-tier operator. He struggled on for four years, but quit after he was widely outpointed in his home town by journeyman Dhafir Smith. So much for the man once nominated as the future of US boxing.

54

★★★

ENZO
WAYNE
MACCARINELLI VS. BRAITHWAITE

JULY 21, 2007	Cardiff International Arena

★★★

They billed this one as 'Big Macc' against 'Big Truck'. And, with both men's punches equally deserving of the adjective, there were few who expected their collision to be other than brief and explosive. "Don't blink in this one," warned the headline on the preview in *Boxing News*. It turned out differently.

Maccarinelli first laid hands on the WBO cruiserweight belt at the Millennium Stadium, when a nine-round demolition of former WBC ruler

Maccarinelli unloads on Braithwaite

Enzo gets a lift from a sporting loser

Marcelo Domínguez brought him interim ownership. When long-serving champion Johnny Nelson was forced to concede that a troublesome knee injury meant permanent retirement, the Swansea man was elevated to full honours.

His first two defences had ended inside a round. Yorkshireman Mark Hobson, who had taken Enzo all the way seven months earlier, was despatched in 71 seconds, while colourful Canadian Bobby Gunn lasted only a little longer.

Wayne Braithwaite came with rather more impressive credentials: after all, he halted 'Buster' Douglas in his first pro fight and saw off Lennox Lewis in his second. Admittedly, these were not the world champions – and neither was the Richard Woodhall he stopped a few years later. But after leaving his native Guyana to settle in Brooklyn, Wayne met some genuine top-class operators before knocking out another US-based West Indian, the previously unbeaten Louis Azille, to clinch a crack at the WBC cruiser throne.

He had to travel to Italy for his big chance, but that was no problem to Braithwaite, who had won twice in Australia to add to his Caribbean and American successes. He battered local hero Vincenzo Cantatore to a 10th-round stoppage, defending three times before losing unanimously in a unification clash with France's excellent WBA king, Jean-Marc Mormeck.

A second straight loss, at the hands of Guillermo Jones, a Panamanian who had held Nelson to a draw, suggested a new vulnerablity, and Braithwaite took 18 months out, but returned with a stoppage win before heading for Wales.

Perhaps it was a mutual respect for each other's power, but the pair were content to box in the opening stages, Maccarinelli seemingly unfazed by the challenger's switch-hitting tactics. And when solid blows were unleashed, those fired by the Welshman looked to have more impact than the shots coming the other way.

Braithwaite greeted them with mock staggers, sticking out his tongue in one of those "you didn't hurt me" gestures that often indicate the opposite. There was no way for Wayne to disguise the effect of the hooking combination which put him down in the fifth, but the bell came to his rescue.

The adopted New Yorker had his moments when he turned southpaw and used his jab, but they were brief interludes in Enzo's domination. A right uppercut brought blood from Braithwaite's mouth and there were several occasions during the closing rounds when Wayne looked about to fold. He gritted his teeth, however, and saw it out, only to find that one judge had given every session to Maccarinelli. The two others were marginally more lenient, but the champion could celebrate perhaps the best performance of his career.

Braithwaite bounced back to stop unbeaten Cuban Yoan Pablo Hernández in Germany, but a couple of 2012 losses back home in Georgetown prompted him to hand up his gloves.

Maccarinelli repelled one more challenger before suffering a shattering defeat inside two rounds in an attempt to unify the division against WBC and WBA boss David Haye. It marked the start of a rocky road, with further stoppage losses prompting calls from many – including promoter Frank Warren – for him to call it a day.

The Swansea man demurred, picking up British and European crowns before dropping to light-heavy, where he was prematurely halted by Ovill McKenzie in a Commonwealth title tilt. When they met again, Enzo won a thriller, and went on to challenge for a second world crown, only for a horrendously swollen eye to wreck his bout with WBA ruler Jürgen Brähmer.

55

★★★

JOE
vs.
BERNARD
CALZAGHE
HOPKINS

| APRIL 19, 2008 | Thomas and Mack Arena, Las Vegas |

★★★

O ccasionally, the world of sport produces someone whose achievements exceed all normal expectations. While outstanding practitioners of their chosen craft, these rare creatures stand out not merely through the heights they have reached, but because of a longevity rarely seen in activities which rely so crucially on physical fitness.

Writers, actors and singers can stay at the top for half a century or more, but the careers of athletes are notoriously brief. In no other field is a performer routinely referred to as a veteran once past the age of 30.

Yet even here some defy Father Time. Stanley Matthews played in the Football League at 50, cricketer Wilfred Rhodes appeared in his final Test match at 52 and sprinter Merlene Ottey competed internationally at the same age.

And boxing, where the body takes an extra helping of physical punishment, has, nonetheless, its own Methuselahs. George Foreman regained the world heavyweight title at 45, while former WBC light-welter king Saoul Mamby, dethroned in 1982, had his last bout 26 years later when

The Battle of the Planet: Las Vegas prepares

he was 60 years old. Domestically, Barbados-born Londoner Sam Minto boxed in five different decades.

Yet there is nobody comparable to Bernard Hopkins. The Philadelphian who calls himself 'The Executioner' has been fighting for world crowns regularly over more than 20 years. He first challenged for the IBF middle title in May 1993, losing to Roy Jones, Jr. But he went on to claim that belt, defending it 18 times and adding the other three major versions to consolidate his superiority.

After being dethroned by Jermain Taylor, 'B-Hop' jumped two divisions to light-heavy, defeating Antonio Tarver to acquire a couple of minor straps and, more prestigiously, *Ring* magazine recognition as the best at his new weight. Then along came Joe Calzaghe.

Nose to nose – no love lost here

The Newbridge southpaw was also moving up. He had surpassed Hopkins's record with 21 defences of the WBO super-middle honour, gathering the WBC and IBF varieties along the way. And he was still unbeaten. Yet somehow he had never been accorded the worldwide respect given Bernard, despite the latter's four losses. Surely, beating the legend would end that anomaly.

It was not Calzaghe's fault – nor that of promoter Frank Warren – that the pair had not met before. A deal was done for Hopkins to fly to Britain and

The Welsh turn out in force for the weigh-in

Joe takes an unscheduled trip to the canvas

challenge for Joe's super-middle honours; the following day the American rang back to ask for double the money agreed. But a nose-to-nose row in a Las Vegas press room before Ricky Hatton's December 2007 fight with Floyd Mayweather revived public interest, particularly when Hopkins insisted, "I'll never let a white boy beat me."

With Bernard more realistic in his financial demands – and Joe willing to go to the US – the fight was finally made.

Calzaghe did not travel alone, either. Maybe not the army who followed Hatton, but enough accompanied Joe to Sin City to make themselves heard, particularly at the weigh-in at Planet Hollywood. The stars came out, too.

Sylvester Stallone, Bruce Willis and Arnold Schwarzenegger shared ringside seats with Welsh celebrities such as Ioan Gruffudd and Catherine Zeta-Jones, draped in the national flag. And Sir Tom Jones, a daffodil in his lapel, climbed through the ropes to sing *Hen Wlad fy Nhadau*.

The fight began to chants of "Super, super Joe, super Joe Calzaghe", but within a minute their subject found himself on the canvas. Hopkins uncorked a sharp right as his rival moved in and Joe was dropped, shock written all over his face. He was up by the time referee Joe Cortez – the man in charge when Calzaghe beat Chris Eubank more than a decade earlier – had reached the count of three. But a 10-8 round gave the 43-year-old a flying start.

The setback did not deflect Joe from his gameplan. Constantly moving forward, he attempted to draw Hopkins into the sort of exchanges the crowd had hoped to see. But 'B-Hop' did not remain at the top for so long by indulging in tear-ups; pleasing the fans was not high among his priorities. And his elusive, spoiling tactics – he was quick to pin Calzaghe's right arm,

NEVADA STATE ATHLETIC COMMISSION
OFFICIAL SCORE CARD

Title:	Ring Magazine World Light Heavyweight	Referee:	Joe Cortez
Date:	4/19/2008 City: Las Vegas	Venue:	Thomas & Mack Center
Bout: 5	WHITE	Promoter:	Golden Boy Promotions/Don Chargin Productions

Bernard Hopkins (A)			Round	Joe Calzaghe (B)		Bernard Hopkins (A)			Round	Joe Calzaghe (B)		Bernard Hopkins (A)			Round	Joe Calzaghe (B)	
Points	Score	Total		Score	Total	Points	Score	Total		Score	Total	Points	Score	Total		Score	Total
	10		1		9		10		1		8		10		1		9
	9	19	2	18	10		10	20	2	17	9		10	20	2	17	9
	10	29	3	27	9		9	29	3	27	10		9	29	3	27	10
	10	39	4	36	9		9	38	4	37	10		9	38	4	37	10
	9	48	5	46	10		9	47	5	46	10		9	47	5	47	10
	9	57	6	56	10		10	58	6	55	9		9	56	6	57	10
	9	66	7	66	10		9	67	7	65	10		9	65	7	67	10
	9	75	8	76	10		9	76	8	75	10		9	74	8	77	10
	9	84	9	86	10		9	85	9	85	10		9	83	9	87	10
	9	93	10	96	10		10	95	10	94	9		9	92	10	97	10
	10	103	11	105	9		10	105	11	103	9		10	102	11	106	9
	9	112	12	115	10		9	114	12	113	10		9	111	12	116	10
		112		115				114		113				111		116	

Judge: Ted Gimza	Judge: Adalaide Byrd	Judge: Chuck Giampa
Suspensions:	Explain deduction of points or comments:	Decision: Calzaghe won by split decision

How the judges saw things

while landing rights of his own – allowed him to score the more telling blows in the early rounds.

Yet the Welshman was busier and the tussle between quantity and quality was reflected in the judges' minds: in none of the five rounds from second to sixth did the trio agree on a winner. Things became clearer as the older man tired and Joe took the seventh, eighth, ninth and last for all three arbiters.

Hopkins used his experience to influence the officials wherever possible. From the second session, he was complaining of low blows and in the tenth dropped to all fours, grimacing, after what replays showed was more a pat than a punch. Calzaghe watched, bemused, for more than a minute as Bernard played to the gallery; the gallery, populated largely by Welshmen, was unimpressed, a chorus of "Cheat! Cheat!" filling the air.

The American repeated his antics in the next, but Cortez sternly ordered him to box on. He nevertheless took the round, creating enough uncertainty in the Calzaghe corner for trainer Enzo to urge his son to make the scorecards redundant.

Hopkins snubbed the customary glove-touch before the final stanza, yet was willing enough to use his fists in less ceremonial fashion. But Joe had the better of the exchanges and raised his arms in perceived triumph before closing the contest with a barrage that saw the referee having to drag him away at the gong. There was no mid-ring embrace; instead, the fighters barely glanced at each other as they waited for MC Michael Buffer, back at work a week after treatment for throat cancer, to pronounce the verdict.

The first score announced was that of Adalaide Byrd, who saw it 114-113 for Hopkins. Ted Gimza cancelled that out with 115-112 in favour of Calzaghe. And Chuck Giampa's 116-111 prompted a leap of triumph from the victorious Welshman. And the CompuBox stats underlined that the right man had got the nod: Joe had landed 232 punches, more than anyone had managed before against 'The Executioner'.

While Joe used Max Kellerman's in-ring interview to pay due tribute to Hopkins, his opponent was the epitome of the sore loser. At the post-fight press conference, he railed at the judges, insisting, "I don't think Calzaghe won. He got the victory, that's all." And, still without even a nod in the Welshman's direction, he and his fawning family stalked from the room.

For Joe, there was to be just one more performance before retirement. For Hopkins, the story was far from over. At 46, he defeated Canadian Jean Pascal to win the WBC light-heavy belt. Even losing it a year later to Chad Dawson did not signal the end, and March 2013 saw him take the IBF title from Tavoris Cloud and become, at 48, the oldest man ever to win a world championship.

56

★★★

GARY
LOCKETT

VS.

KELLY
PAVLIK

| JUNE 7, 2008 | Boardwalk Hall, Atlantic City |

★★★

Gary Lockett always had a pragmatic relationship with boxing. The builder's son from Cwmbran discovered at an early age that he could knock opponents out and worked hard to graft a solid technique on to his natural power. When he turned pro it was a decision driven by a desire for financial security rather than a lust for glory.

It had been a successful move, with only one defeat, later avenged, along with the acquisition of a couple of minor belts, including the lightly regarded WBU version of the world middleweight title. After all, the 12-round fights involved meant bigger paydays. It was time to cash in and get out. And that coincided with the rise of Kelly Pavlik.

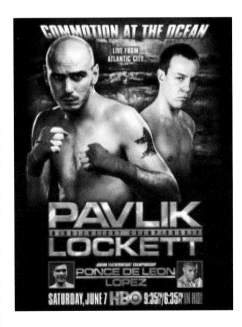

The shaven-headed slugger from the Ohio steel city of Youngstown was the first American boxer to attract the sort of travelling support that is common in Europe. Thousands of blue-collar fans regularly followed him to fights in Atlantic City.

A former junior champion, Kelly's aggressive style guaranteed excitement and only three of his 31 pro victims had lasted the course when he climbed through the ropes at the Boardwalk Hall to challenge WBC and WBO middleweight champion Jermain Taylor. In a thriller which captivated those seeing him for the first time, Pavlik recovered from a second-round knockdown to halt Taylor in the seventh, while still behind on the cards.

The triumph, and the manner of it, was a boost for Youngstown, the city with the lowest average income in the US. That background reinforced Pavlik's impact on public consciousness; he became "flavour of the month" on the American fight scene.

A rematch clause meant he and Taylor met again – Kelly won a catchweight contest on points – but with that contractual obligation out of the way, he (and TV giants HBO) were on the lookout for a viable first challenger, preferably someone who would not kill the new golden goose.

They looked to the east and came up with Lockett. The Welshman knew exactly why he had been selected. Unlike many boxers, he was fully aware of the quasi-political machinations behind the sport. He had, in fact, been offered a shot at IBF champion Arthur Abraham, but the payday came with conditions: if he won, Gary would have to make up to five defences for the German promoter.

The Pavlik option, while a tougher task, paid around four times as much, although it needed his signature on a new contract with Frank Warren to secure the engagement. With his business head on, the Welshman agreed to accept the role of sacrificial lamb.

"I knew I was up against it," says Gary. "My only chance was to land a big punch before he did."

Lockett has his moments early on

Having sought inspiration in tapes of Lloyd Honeyghan's unexpected dethronement of Don Curry in 1986, Lockett knew he had to come out blasting. It never happened. Instead, he found that Pavlik, significantly taller and naturally bigger, was difficult to reach. And an early shot which brought blood from the Welshman's nose underlined the venom in the champion's gloves.

Gary's own blows seemed merely to provoke Kelly into stepping up his replies and a flurry in the second saw the challenger take a knee. He rose at eight and tried to fight back as Pavlik went for the finish, only to ship a big right which dropped him once more. This time the bell came to his assistance.

Pavlik knows it's nearly over

It merely delayed the inevitable, however. Lockett launched a desperate assault to open the third, but the American brushed it aside and a right to the temple sent him staggering backwards before again dropping to one knee. Although he clambered up at nine, trainer Enzo Calzaghe and referee Eddie Cotton agreed it was time to end it.

For Pavlik it was supposedly another step on the road to superstardom. But four months later he was overwhelmingly outpointed by Bernard Hopkins and, although he had a second spell as champion, a battle with alcoholism derailed that particular dream.

Lockett, however, banked the cheque and promptly turned his back on a sport he professed never to love, preferring to focus on his property portfolio and other business interests. But boxing is not a mistress so easily spurned: a year later Gary took out a trainer's licence, later becoming a manager as well. Less than five years after his first visit to Atlantic City, he was back at the Boardwalk Hall in the corner of another Welsh world title challenger, lightweight Gavin Rees.

57

The man in the front row was emphatic. "Calzaghe is getting his backside handed to him," he laughed into his mobile phone. "Jones is taking him to school."

If he had made the call after the first round, when Joe, for the second time in two visits to the States, was on the canvas, the comment might have been understandable. But, with four rounds gone, it merely showed how little one ringsider understood what was happening in front of him.

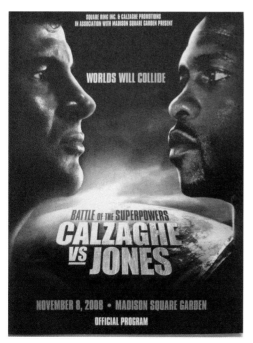

Much had happened in the life of Joe Calzaghe since his victory over Bernard Hopkins seven months earlier. He had relinquished his super-middle belts, acknowledging that he would never again make 12st (168lb). And he had split, acrimoniously, with Frank Warren, the man who had promoted him for the past dozen years.

Cutting out the middle men, Calzaghe and Roy Jones, Jr, had met privately to agree terms between them. For the American, it was an opportunity to reclaim a place among the world's best after recent setbacks. For Joe, it would be the climax to an extraordinary career.

Not that many CVs could match that of his final foe. The man from Pensacola, Florida, had been awarded the Val Barker Trophy as the best boxer in the Seoul Olympics, despite being robbed against a local in the final by a trio of judges later found to have been wined and dined by Korean officials. That single outrageous result was largely responsible for amateur boxing's adoption of computer scoring.

Jones's switch to the paid ranks saw him collect world titles at middle, super-middle and light-heavy before, incredibly, outclassing WBA ruler John Ruiz to claim a heavyweight belt as well. He returned to his natural light-heavy class but, after just one defeat, via controversial disqualification, in his first 50 contests, he was stopped by former victim Antonio Tarver, an achievement repeated by eternal contender Glen Johnson. Perhaps the excursion into the heavyweights and the enforced weight

Roy Jones, Jr, and a few of his belts

loss afterwards had taken its toll; whatever the reason, Roy was no longer unbeatable.

But he had just won three 12-rounders in a row, most recently widely outpointing hall-of-fame candidate Félix Trinidad. He was far from finished when he and Calzaghe crossed gloves in the legendary Garden.

Certainly, many tipped Jones to win, among them, perhaps inevitably, mutual opponent Hopkins. Even Joe's 11-year-old son, Connor, after watching tapes of Roy in his prime, had pleaded with his father not to fight him.

The youngster, at ringside with his older brother, Joe, Jr, found no reassurance in the opening exchanges. The 14,000 fans at the iconic venue above Penn Station gasped in unison as Jones followed a solid left lead with a right hook which sent Calzaghe to his knees in the centre of the ring. The impact, with forearm supplementing fist, brought blood from the bridge of the Welshman's nose and, when he climbed up at the count of six, he was clearly more shaken than he had been by Hopkins's similar early knockdown.

Joe's head cleared quickly, however, and he went on the attack. Roy seemed unwilling to risk an all-out follow-up and his opportunity was lost.

Calzaghe finishes his career in style

The round, naturally, was his by a 10-8 margin. But none of the three judges gave him anything else as Calzaghe turned on what father Enzo was to describe as the best performance of his career.

His speed and swarming aggression kept Jones focussed on defence and his confidence was such that, as early as the third, he dropped his hands and swayed his hips in the sort of showmanship with which the American had made his name. Roy, his left eye swelling and eventually, from the seventh, pouring blood, was never able to come to terms with his task.

The Florida man's bravery was never in doubt, however. He battled on, encouraged by the success of individual blows, but could never sustain an assault or put the Welshman under real pressure. At the final bell, in contrast to the Hopkins fight, the pair embraced, their mutual respect evident.

Jones continued boxing into his forties; four years later he travelled to Poland to end the unbeaten record of a local hero. But for Calzaghe it was the end of the road. After 46 winning fights, the last 24 for world honours – the Hopkins and Jones bouts did not involve alphabet titles, but the arguably more prestigious *Ring* magazine belt was at stake each time – he hung up his gloves.

He was three short of the 49-bout winning streak set by another world champion who retired undefeated. And Rocky Marciano's younger brother was sure 'The Rock' would have appreciated Joe.

"If he was still here, he'd have loved Calzaghe, I can guarantee that," said Peter Marciano. "Rocky liked the guys that stuck to the business and worked like crazy. And it doesn't hurt that he's Italian!"

58

★★

NATHAN
vs.
CLEVERLY

SHAWN
HAWK

| NOVEMBER 10, 2012 | Staples Center, Los Angeles |

★★

The undefeated Welshman had found that even being a world champion in these days of multiple titles meant little outside his own patch. And his avowed wish to unify the crowns had come up against the traditional unwillingness of American boxers to leave home.

Numerous European and Asian stars have been dissed by US critics for failing to risk their reputations across the Atlantic, with Joe Calzaghe a particular target until the last knockings of his career. But they never aimed similar accusations at such native greats as Oscar de la Hoya, Sugar Ray Leonard, Roy Jones or Floyd Mayweather, none of whom ever laced up a professional glove beyond their national borders.

The efforts of promoter Frank Warren to tempt rival rulers Chad Dawson, Tavoris Cloud or Beibut Shumenov to board a transatlantic flight had met with blank refusal. The same applied to the legendary Bernard Hopkins. Cleverly bowed to the inevitable and opted to chase his prey on its own territory.

Outside the four above – and perhaps Canadian Jean Pascal – there were no instantly recognisable names in the world rankings at light-heavyweight. With none of his main targets prepared to play ball, each announcement of a new challenger for the Cefn Fforest fighter would be greeted with predictable scorn.

It was not Cleverly's fault that German Jürgen

Nathan Cleverly, triple titleholder

Shawn Hawk of the Lakota Sioux

Brähmer's repeated pull-outs led to him being stripped and Nathan's enthronement as full champion without throwing a punch. Sure, two-day substitute Aleksy Kuziemski was not a worthy opponent and duly succumbed in four rounds.

At least Tony Bellew and his unbeaten record meant something in Britain, but while Nathan's victory in front of the Scouser's own fans earned him plaudits at home it barely created a ripple in the US. And even a wide points success over an actual American, Tommy Karpency, went practically unnoticed.

Vyacheslav Uzelkov, nominated to challenge Cleverly in Cardiff in October, proved similarly unappealing, so there was an abrupt change of plan. The home fight was scrapped and Nathan was added to an already top-heavy Golden Boy bill in Los Angeles a fortnight later.

Clearly one of Uncle Sam's boys was needed for the opposite corner, but Ryan Coyne was forced to withdraw in the face of legal threats by promoter Don King. Enter Shawn Hawk. At least both men now had back stories which would garner some publicity in the American media.

Nathan, raised in the Phillipstown area of New Tredegar, had turned from a self-confessed "little thug" into an articulate and courteous university graduate, whose maths degree set him apart from the average pugilist.

Hawk, from a Native American reservation in South Dakota, was a reformed alcoholic who wore an impressive feathered head-dress into the ring.

Cleverly sported his customary bandanna, though only after a last-ditch search of local shops, having forgotten to pack one in his kitbag. But his ringwalk was notable for his companions: singing superstar Sir Tom Jones and Hollywood actor and former pro boxer Mickey Rourke. Such high-profile support attracted headlines – as did the approval of renowned trainer Freddie Roach, following a sparring session at the Wild Card gym – making up for the fight's tea-time scheduling.

Nathan moves in for the finish

Clev and his celebrity fans celebrate

With the Latino fans drawn by the show's main attractions yet to arrive, there were few present in the flesh. But the purpose of the exercise was to introduce Cleverly to the armchair followers across the country and those Showtime subscribers were entertained by what they saw.

Despite the late replacement of the southpaw Coyne by an orthodox fighter, Nathan was in control from the first bell. Hawk quickly began to show the evidence of the Welshman's assault while, although he was able to land occasional shots as Cleverly scorned defence in his eagerness to put on a show, they had no apparent effect on the recipient.

By the middle rounds, the traffic was increasingly one-way and the visitor moved up a gear in the seventh, focussing on the body and twice flooring the 'Sioux Warrior'. Each time Shawn dragged himself upright, but with little conviction. A compassionate corner might have pulled him out at the bell, but he was sent back into the firing line and soon found himself taking another count. Only after another minute's pummelling did referee Tony Crebs call a halt.

The victory took Cleverly's record to 25 straight wins, one for each year of his life. But, more importantly, it introduced a crowd-pleaser to a new fan base and paved the way for bigger challenges down the road.

59

★★★

GAVIN	VS.	ADRIEN
REES		**BRONER**

FEBRUARY 16, 2013	**Boardwalk Hall, Atlantic City**

★★★

Jet lag was never likely to be a problem for Gavin Rees. He arrived in the US more than a month before fight night and based himself in New York to complete his preparation.

There were advantages to compensate for going stir-crazy in a Manhattan apartment. Prior to his arrival, few Stateside had heard of him. OK, he was 32 and a 14-year career had included the WBO light-welter title and British and European reigns in the division below. But he had never faced an American or boxed in a US ring, so those achievements had gone unnoticed by the blinkered locals. Now at least he was able to introduce himself to the East Coast media.

Gavin Rees: moody machismo

Adrien Broner was already familiar to fight fans, in large part the result of his own dedication to making it so. But beyond the hype and the histrionics, at 23 the Cincinnati kid had already achieved what Rees was aiming for - world titles at two weights.

The WBO super-feather belt had been followed the previous November by the WBC lightweight crown, removed from the battered head of Mexican hard man Antonio de Marco. Even those pundits immune to Broner's publicity machine were calling him the natural pound-for-pound successor to Floyd Mayweather.

But many disliked the overweening arrogance that was the new star's default setting and preferred the challenger's quiet confidence. The ritual exchange of insults enlivened the pre-fight press conference, although the Welsh camp had the last laugh. When Broner came over to give "Cabbage Rees" one more mouthful as the protagonists left the premises, Gavin replied in kind, so disconcerting the champion that he dropped his phone, which smashed to smithereens.

The mind games continued at the weigh-in, with Adrien supping a can of Sprite as he walked to the scales and the challenger grabbing the belt from one of Broner's acolytes as they posed for pictures.

Rees grabs Broner's belt at the weigh-in

Come the night, Rees looked calm and focussed as he strolled to the ring, contrasting with the pantomime when the American followed, wearing a garish fringed jacket and a head mic, rapping along with his personal praise singer. But, once perma-tanned MC Michael Buffer had invited those present to "Get Ready to Rumble", it was soon clear that Gavin was far from overawed,

He moved in and out, landing repeatedly on a lethargic Broner and awakening a murmur of interest from the crowd. A fast left counter by the holder served as a warning of what was to follow, but it was the Welshman's round. The second, too, saw Rees on the front foot and, after Adrien wound up and landed a bolo punch, 'The Rock' caught him with a left hook as the American dropped his guard.

But it was already clear that the greater power lay in Broner's fists. The challenger was still scoring his share in the third, but he was being picked off with fast and accurate shots and looked worried at the bell.

The fourth proved the decisive session. A vicious right uppercut exploded on Gavin's chin and sent him backwards on to the seat of his pants. Up at four, he recovered well and hurled desperate punches at his tormentor, but Adrien ignored them and forced the Welshman backwards for the first time.

The interval saw trainer Gary Lockett tell his friend and student that he was taking too much, but when referee Earl Brown walked over to check he was told that Rees would continue. Meanwhile, his girlfriend, Kayleigh Jenkins, left her ringside seat to avoid witnessing the inevitable.

Gavin must have been equally certain of what was to follow, but went out bravely to meet Broner toe to toe, though the champion merely shook

Broner attacks - and, as usual, his mouth is open

his head and awaited his opportunity. When Adrien landed a right, Rees attempted his own showboating response, throwing his arms wide in a "That all you got?" gesture; unfortunately, he was still within range and took another solid right from his scornful foe.

As they came together, Broner pushed Rees's head down, prompting a rebuke from the third man. Gavin, perhaps expecting the lecture to last longer, relaxed his guard and shipped a vicious left to the midriff, sending him down for a second count. When Broner redoubled his efforts, driving the Welshman back to the ropes, Lockett stepped on to the ring apron and waved the towel in surrender. Mr Brown stepped between them with one second left of the round.

The victor and self-styled superstar-elect gave a typically bombastic in-ring interview to HBO – having had his hair brushed by a hanger-on beforehand – apologising for not giving the viewers that much to see. But when he joined Rees before the Sky cameras later, he was surprisingly respectful to the Welshman.

Nevertheless, it was something he said during the first chat which summed up the fight. "It was a matter of levels," said Broner. And, for all Gavin's determination and courage, that undeniable fact remained: the American was, indeed, in a different class.

60

NATHAN **CLEVERLY**	VS.	SERGEY **KOVALEV**
AUGUST 17, 2013		Motorpoint Arena, Cardiff

With unification fights unforthcoming, the Welshman scoured the rankings for a challenger who would stir the interest of experts across the Atlantic, while silencing growing criticism at home. He came up with a Florida-based Russian with power in both fists.

Sergey Kovalev had left his native Chelyabinsk to settle in the States when he turned pro in 2009 and won his first nine bouts inside two rounds, campaigning across the country at venues ranging from a gym in Atlanta to the Playboy Mansion in Beverly Hills. When he halted former WBA champion Gabriel Campillo in three it earned him a world ranking – and piqued the interest of TV giants HBO.

But just as the new flavour of the month was about to sign on the dotted line for a visit to Wales, the plot took a sudden twist. Former Cleverly victim Karo Murat, mandatory challenger to IBF boss Bernard Hopkins, was refused a visa to enter the US, just as Kovalev thrashed once-beaten Cornelius White to earn prompt recognition as Murat's replacement at No 1.

Even when the German-based Serb's visa problems were suddenly sorted, the IBF stuck with Kovalev and it seemed likely that Sergey would opt for the higher-profile shot at Hopkins. But, with B-Hop non-committal and neither HBO

The fearsome Kovalev (left) gives Cleverly the eye

The Florida-based Russian is so close to the title

nor rivals Showtime particularly keen on showing the contest, the Russian and his promoters, Main Events, plumped for the bird in the hand and signed to box in Cardiff.

The visitor, trained by double world champion John David Jackson, was promptly installed as favourite, the odds-makers clearly impressed by the power reflected in a record of 19 stoppages from 21 victories, all but one of them coming in the first three rounds. Those fans who had checked out Kovalev's fights on YouTube tended to agree with the bookies. More optimistic observers pointed out that Sergey had never been beyond eight rounds, hoping that Cleverly's speed and mobility would win out if he survived the early onslaught.

The first session saw Nathan keeping his left jab working, using his significant reach advantage, while defending effectively when Kovalev unfurled his hooks. The second saw the challenger nicked by the right eye; he then let his mouthpiece fall to the floor. Yet he looked relaxed and ominously untroubled.

Midway through the third, a right and a solid left uppercut rocked Cleverly. When Sergey landed two more rights, the second landing behind the ear, it sent Nathan briefly to the canvas. He rose, perhaps too quickly, but Kovalev scented blood. Another barrage returned the champion to the deck – he shipped a couple more while there - and his legs were still shaky as referee Terry O'Connor waved the pair back into action.

Cleverly was all over the place as the round ended, stumbling into the Brummie official, who grabbed him round the waist. It looked as if he was calling a halt, but the bell rang at that second and O'Connor instead directed the wobbling Welshman to his corner. It was a brief reprieve.

Just 29 seconds into the fourth, Nathan was clipped by a left hook, half-toppling forward and touching the canvas with both gloves. There was no point in taking up the count. His two-year reign was over.

As the delirious Russians celebrated the arrival of a new star on the world stage, the heartbroken Cleverly sat disconsolately on his stool. He took a few months off "to lead a normal life" before deciding to box on as a cruiserweight.

61

OVER HERE

The Welsh-American connection dates back to the dawn of organised boxing. And many of the early champions made sure that this small nation to the left of England was on their itineraries when they cashed in on their celebrity with public appearances in Europe.

Back at the tail-end of the Victorian era, the world heavyweight title was considered the greatest prize in sport. Its holders were the shining stars of the athletic world. And Welsh audiences were as keen as any to see their idols at close quarters.

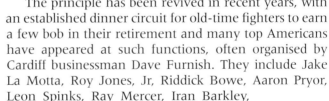

John L. Sullivan visited Cardiff in 1887, attracting bigger crowds than Prime Minister Gladstone. Bob Fitzsimmons, Cornish-born, but by then a US citizen, boxed exhibitions in the city in 1896. Early in the new century, Jack Johnson stayed at the Ruperra Hotel in Pontypridd, a well-known boxers' haunt, while he was on tour.

The principle has been revived in recent years, with an established dinner circuit for old-time fighters to earn a few bob in their retirement and many top Americans have appeared at such functions, often organised by Cardiff businessman Dave Furnish. They include Jake La Motta, Roy Jones, Jr, Riddick Bowe, Aaron Pryor, Leon Spinks, Ray Mercer, Iran Barkley,

Riddick Bowe enjoys his visit to Wales

Ray Mancini, Carmen Basilio, Tim Witherspoon and Sugar Ray Leonard, who was also part of the promotional team when his Contender star, Peter Manfredo, Jr, visited Wales to face Joe Calzaghe at the Millennium Stadium.

On the promotional side, the inimitable Don King enlivened the scene when in partnership with Frank Warren and MCs Michael Buffer and Jimmy Lennon, Jr, have dropped in to announce fights destined for American TV. But there have been others who threw serious punches here.

Perhaps the most famous is Rocky Marciano, whose first knockout is said to have come in South Wales, while he was training with the US Army prior to the D-Day landings in 1943. The story tells of an Australian sailor throwing his

Marciano's bar in Swansea's Adelphi

Joe Louis boxed an exhibition in Newport

weight about and insisting that he "could lick any Yank in the place". Rocky, encouraged by his comrades, promptly decked the braggart with one right hand.

The basic details recur each time the tale is told. But as for where it happened, that depends on who's telling it. Even Rocky himself seemed uncertain; he told fight commentator Reg Gutteridge it was in a pub in Cardiff, but on other occasions claimed it was in Swansea and, according to one biography, wrote to his parents that it all took place in a fish and chip shop. Perhaps he didn't want them to think he'd been out drinking!

As it is, several establishments have been put forward as the scene of Rocky's epiphany. The Baroness Windsor and the Golden Cross, in Cardiff, are two. The Castle Hotel at Maenclochog, in rural Pembrokeshire, has its supporters. Others point to one of the many pubs in Mumbles, while the Adelphi, in Swansea's Wind Street, has a Marciano's Bar and assorted "witness statements" to underline its claim.

Rocky saw some formal ring action while still in Wales, swapping punches with an opponent who was to achieve equally legendary status in the rugby world. Jack Matthews was part of a team of medical students who met a line-up of GIs and emerged with a draw against one Rocco Marchegiano. Only when he saw the world heavyweight ruler's picture in the papers several years later did he realise his foe's identity. Rocky probably never did know that his rival achieved his own immortality as 'Dr Jack', one of the greatest centres Wales has ever seen.

Marciano, of course, ended the career of the incomparable Joe Louis, forced by tax bills to fight on long beyond his sell-by date. The 'Brown Bomber' also appeared in Wales during the war, headlining a fund-raiser in Newport in the summer of 1944. He boxed an exhibition against a fellow-countryman, Master Sergeant Keen Simmons, a former Golden Gloves champion.

Another top heavyweight to visit, this time to box competitively, was 19-year-old Gerry Cooney, whose left hook flattened Newport novice Terry Chard – having only his fourth bout – in 90 seconds to clinch a 4-3 victory for a touring New York amateur team against South Wales at Caerphilly's Club Double Diamond in October 1975.

Chard, twice a Welsh ABA champion, was in good company. Ron Lyle and Ken Norton were both first-round victims before Cooney lost a classic world title challenge to Larry Holmes.

And at least Terry has received a name-check for his part in the long history of Welsh-American fistic relationships.

The teenage Gerry Cooney (right) and New York team-mate Luis Resto in Caerphilly

62

OVER THERE

The transatlantic trade in boxers has not been confined to those crossing the ocean for lucrative shots at major titles. Others, particularly in the first half of the last century, headed west in search of a better life.

Freddie Welsh, the man who took his country's name as his own, is the outstanding example, but there were many others who campaigned at a decent standard. Eddie Morgan and Frank Moody came up against world champions; those encounters are recorded in the main section of this book. But there were others worthy of note.

Gipsy Daniels had already picked up his nickname before sailing to New York in 1922 – because of his dark complexion, rather than his actual heritage – but it was Jim Johnston, the 'Boy Bandit of Broadway', who capitalised on it. Having told the press that the Llanelli man was a Romany prince, the supreme publicist went on board with big brass ear-rings, a yellow silk bandanna around his head, loose velvet trousers and an embroidered coat for him to wear as he disembarked.

It did the trick: Daniels became very popular, winning eight of his nine contests before returning to Europe, where he later knocked out Max Schmeling inside a round as well as becoming British champion.

Promoters in that era often sought to recruit talented Welsh fighters, such was their reputation for entertaining the punters. This was particularly the case in Pennsylvania, where thousands of unemployed miners had escaped from the hardship of the Valleys.

One such promoter was Frank Torreyson, who asked Cardiff journalist Charlie Barnett to select a couple of likely lads. The first name he recommended was a tiny terror who was knocking everyone out; Torreyson rejected him as too small to

Gipsy Daniels, as transformed by 'The Boy Bandit'

Fred Dyer, boxer and baritone

appeal to American crowds. Instead Barnett chose two Rhondda boys, Les Williams and Dai Bowen; the pair were lost with the *Titanic*. The lucky youngster who stayed at home was Jimmy Wilde, who went on to dazzle US observers when he finally made the crossing a few years later.

The migrant miners themselves produced some useful boxers. Perhaps the best was Willie Davies, who left Maesteg when his father headed for the Pennsylvania coalfield. Willie went on to enjoy a 10-year career which saw him battle the likes of Midget Wolgast, Frankie Genaro and Emile Pladner.

One of the most colourful characters to appear in the US was Fred Dyer, a Cardiffian known worldwide as 'The Singing Boxer'. Renowned for serenading the fans after his fights, Dyer arrived in the US from Australia in 1916 and travelled the country, performing on stage as well as in the ring. By the end of World War I he was training American soldiers at Camp Grant.

A pair of Welsh-Italian brothers from Pontypridd provide contrasting stories. Walter Rossi sailed west as a teenager, learned the basics and returned to win a Welsh title; younger brother Francis, who once drew with the legendary Jim Driscoll, ended his career Stateside, where he took out citizenship and remained until his death.

In the 1940s Cyril Gallie, a former amateur star whose peak years were lost to World War II, made a belated switch to the pros and became a big attraction at New York's Broadway Arena, one scribe calling him "the best pound-for-pound fighter I've ever seen". He did lose three of his nine bouts in the US, but that comment suggests they thought he was a bit special, nonetheless.

More recently, the country offered an attractive option for those who found their

Winston Burnett crossed the Atlantic to reach 100 fights

livelihood curtailed by the British Board's increasingly strict medical requirements. Cardiff journeyman Winston Burnett was left stranded on 99 fights when his licence was pulled after he suffered a detached retina; he promptly headed for Indianapolis, called himself J.W. St Clair, and had another couple of dozen contests.

Former British heavyweight champion David Pearce was less successful in avoiding detection. Banned at home after a brain scan had revealed anomalies, he reappeared after six years' inactivity to fight in Michigan. The Newport man looked awful as he was

Dai Dollings, in his eighties, massages fighter Al Reid

halted in eight rounds by the obese Percell Davis and the state authorities, having now been informed of the British suspension, instituted their own ban.

In this century, Merthyr cruiserweight Dean Williams campaigned in the US under the management of former world heavyweight boss Larry Holmes, while fellow-townsman Kerry Hope and Swansea's James Todd moved to Los Angeles in a bid to boost their careers, but both returned after a few months.

Occasionally, Welsh amateurs have caught the eye in the US. When Albert Barnes beat future world champion Petey Scalzo in New York in 1935 – featured elsewhere in the book - his great Cardiffian mate and rival, Jackie Pottinger, was also on the GB team. And it was in Houston in 1999 that Carmarthen heavyweight Kevin Evans became the first British boxer to win a medal at a world amateur championships.

But one of the most successful Welshmen on the American fight scene was not a boxer at all. Dai Dollings, born in Swansea in 1867, was a useful bareknuckle practitioner in his youth. He turned to training and was soon in demand on both sides of the Atlantic, but became particularly famous at New York's Grupps Gym, where he looked after champions including Johnny Dundee and Jack Britton.

He also mentored a young Ray Arcel, later to become one of the most brilliant trainers in history, while veteran manager Tom O'Rourke called Dai "the greatest man in boxing". Perhaps it's about time he had some real recognition in his homeland.

BIBLIOGRAPHY

The following are among many publications consulted during the writing of this book:

Sporting Life, Mirror of Life, Boxing, Boxing News, Boxing Monthly, The Ring, Boxing Illustrated, Western Mail, South Wales Echo, South Wales Daily News, South Wales Evening Post.
Wales and its Boxers, ed. Peter Stead and Gareth Williams (University of Wales)
Fighting was my Business, by Jimmy Wilde (Robson)
Occupation: Prizefighter, The Freddie Welsh Story, by Andrew Gallimore (Seren)
Thus Farr, by Tommy Farr (Optomen)
A Welshman in the Bronx, by Graeme Kent (Gomer)
Man of Courage, by Bob Lonkhurst (Book Guild)
No Ordinary Joe, by Joe Calzaghe (Century)
A Fighting Life, by Enzo Calzaghe (Great Northern)
Johnny! The Story of the Happy Warrior, by Alan Roderick (Heron)
A Bloody Canvas, The Mike McTigue Story, by Andrew Gallimore (Mercier)
All in my Corner, by Tony Lee (TL Associates)
The Jewish Boxers' Hall of Fame, by Ken Blady (Shapolsky)
The 100 Greatest Boxers of All Time, by Bert Randolph Sugar (Bonanza)
The following websites were also useful sources of information:
boxrec.com, Welsh Warriors, www.boxinghistory.org.uk, Amateur Boxing Results, www.fultonhistory.com, Wikipedia.